JB JOSSEY-BASS™
A Wiley Brand

138 Ways to Generate New, First-time Gifts

Scott C. Stevenson, Editor

WILEY

978-1-118-69175-5   ISBN

978-1-118-70377-9   ISBN (online)

138 Ways to Generate New, First-time Gifts

Published by

Stevenson, Inc.

P.O. Box 4528 • Sioux City, Iowa • 51104

Phone 712.239.3010 • Fax 712.239.2166

www.stevensoninc.com

138 Ways to Generate New, First-time Gifts

TABLE OF CONTENTS

138 Ways to Generate New, First-time Gifts

TABLE OF CONTENTS

138 Ways to Generate New, First-time Gifts

1 Fundraising Video Connects Supporters

Every April the Mercer Island Schools Foundation (Mercer Island, WA) hosts its Community & Business Leaders Breakfast.

Less than an hour after it begins, the event is over and the foundation has raised almost a half-million dollars ($430,000 in 2009), thanks in large part to specially produced videos featuring students, teachers and foundation-funded programs.

"With the brevity of the fundraiser, we really have to touch people in a powerful and meaningful way," says Penny Yantis, executive director of the foundation. "The videos create that heart-and-soul emotional pull more effectively than almost anything else we could program."

Foundation officials produce one video a year. A four-person committee working directly with a professional videographer sets the film's theme and focus.

Once interview questions are crafted, filming takes just three or four days, but that is just the first step in a hectic process, Yantis says. Two months of editing, reviewing and re-editing is what brings the video into focus.

Yantis says the $7,000 cost to produce each video is well worth it.

"Emotional impact is what draws people in, and this allows us to tell our story in a very compelling way," she says. "The films really connect community leaders to the people and programs they would be supporting."

Check out the videos at http://mercerislandschoolsfoundation.com/impact.

Source: Penny Yantis, Executive Director, Mercer Island Schools Foundation, Mercer Island, WA. Phone (206) 275-2550. E-mail: payantis@hotmail.com

2 Try Testing Back-to-back Appeals

Think of all the junk mail you receive at home. Much of it hardly gets a glance before it's off to the trash. And sometimes mail you may have read in other circumstances — more time on your hands, less stressed, etc. — gets lumped in with the junk mail.

That's the same way many of those to whom you send an appeal might react. Under some circumstances your letter will get pitched without even having been opened, while in others, the recipient might read it and positively respond with a gift. That's why you should periodically test back-to-back mailings to the same group.

Send an appeal to a smaller segment of your mailing list. Then, say 30 or 45 days later, send another appeal to those in the same group who didn't respond to the first mailing. Begin the second letter with a message such as, "Just in case you missed our first invitation to support an important and deserving project...."

Measure the response of both mailings. Evaluate items such as percentage who responded with a gift to each mailing, average gift size, number of responses, amount generated from each mailing, cost/revenue ratio, etc. Then weigh those stats against any negative responses you received from those who received two mailings in a row.

By testing back-to-back appeals with smaller groups, you can determine whether to use that method for a larger scale campaign.

Follow-up Appeal Messages

Use follow-up messages on both your outer envelope and your letter's opening statement....

✓ We missed hearing back from you.

✓ Your absence was noticed.

✓ It won't be the same without your participation.

✓ Just in case you overlooked our first invitation....

3 Encourage Donors to Host a Reception

Imagine what you could accomplish if 50 of your loyal donors hosted a meal or reception at their homes or offices on behalf of your nonprofit and invited their friends, relatives and associates.

Think of the potential for friend-building and fund-building this outreach effort would have.

Now, take steps to make the concept a reality for your organization by:

1. **Developing a prototype that can be duplicated by others.** Work with a handful of current donors who are willing to host an event. Explain that, in addition to helping them coordinate their individual events, you plan to use them as an example for others to emulate.

2. **Recording as you execute.** As you assist your initial hosts, assemble a how-to procedural document that others can use. Include sample invitations, checklists, catering menus/costs and so forth that can be used as a guide by future hosts.

3. **Inviting your entire donor pool to join in the fun.** Publicize your prototype events. Show others how they work and how those events are helping your organization. Make it as easy as possible for would-be hosts to follow suit.

4 Keeping Challenge Simple Offers Big Gain

The challenge was a simple one — if 10,000 donors made a gift of any amount to Skidmore College (Saratoga, NY) by May 31, 2010, Susan Kettering Williamson, trustee and cochair of the Creative Thought, Bold Promise campaign would add $1 million to her own gift.

The idea was to increase the number of donors giving to Skidmore, and the effort worked, says Lori Eastman, director of development, who says, "One out of four of our donors today did not make gifts to Skidmore last year."

Development staff started marketing the challenge in September 2009 through communications efforts, volunteer programs and student calling. They increased Web and e-mail outreach to include both monthly challenge updates and additional online appeal reminders.

Helping boost those efforts were more than 125 new alumni volunteers who helped reach out to prospective donors, says Eastman. "That gave us the opportunity to contact an additional 1,000-plus classmates with peer-to-peer outreach. One of our graduates was so enthusiastic about the challenge, he offered to help us with a marketing and communications effort."

In the end, the college received gifts from 11,215 donors and secured the $1 million challenge gift. Eastman says it is the simplicity that made the most difference. "It's very important to keep it simple. We were helped by the fact that there wasn't a complicated formula to having gifts matched."

Source: Lori Eastman, Director of Development, Skidmore College, Saratoga Springs, NY. Phone (518) 580-5647. E-mail: leastman@skidmore.edu

5 Benches Offer Beautiful and Comfortable Memorial

"When our campus looks good, we look good," says Maria Clark, administrative assistant for advancement, Oklahoma Christian University (Oklahoma City, OK).

That simple truth is a major motivator for the university's memorial bench program. Building community is another inspiration for the effort, says Clark.

"It was a natural initiative in our effort to make our campus more attractive, comfortable and student- and visitor-friendly," she says.

The pledge for each bench is $1,500, which covers the cost of the bench, a bronze plaque to memorialize or honor someone of the donor's choosing, and funding for a maintenance endowment specifically for the bench program.

Clark says the endowment is important because maintenance has proven to be one of the most challenging parts of the program.

"Our benches are made of teakwood and need to be treated twice a year. We are currently looking at switching to a new bench to help lower the number of man hours needed to keep the benches in top shape. The benches are important to many people, and we want them to look their best all year long."

Another important consideration is planning where the benches will go, she adds. To date, 70 benches have been pledged and nine more are waiting to be placed across campus.

Source: Maria Clark, Administrative Assistant for Advancement, Oklahoma Christian University, Oklahoma City, OK. Phone (405) 425-5094. E-mail: maria.clark@oc.edu

6 Soliciting First-time Gifts

Need direction soliciting first-time gifts? Here are recommendations from *Successful Fund Raising* subscribers:

✓ Cultivate a relationship before soliciting a gift.
✓ Listen to people's ideas to find out where their hearts are.
✓ Complete prospect research before making the contact. If a file exists, read it.
✓ Focus first-time calls on participation rather than going for a gift.
✓ Develop a way of simply stating your nonprofit's mission with which the individual can personally identify.
✓ Know your nonprofit's case thoroughly, and be prepared to respond knowledgeably.
✓ Be honest in describing the use of contributions.
✓ Be yourself and be respectful.
✓ Recognize prospects' unique ability to help others.
✓ Clearly express your nonprofit's needs.
✓ Offer the donor the opportunity to contribute a gift that addresses his/her interests.
✓ Be professional in your initial approach — set an appointment and confirm it with a letter.
✓ Be accompanied, when possible, by someone who knows both the prospect and your nonprofit.
✓ Don't push your own agenda.
✓ Point out the benefits of your organization to them.
✓ Make eye contact and speak with enthusiasm and confidence.

7 Make the Most Of Cold Calls

Cold calls can be intimidating to all levels of development professionals. But sometimes, cold calls are the only means of making contact with new prospects.

To improve your cold-call success rate, follow these three practices:

1. **View your initial call as friend raising.** Use that first-time meeting to get to know each other rather than feeling pressured to secure a gift. Find out more about the prospect and convey key messages about your organization and its mission.

2. **Look for connections from which you can build.** What common interests exist between the prospect and your organization? Has he/she benefitted from its services? Is he/she close to board members or employees? Is it simply the fact that your organization and his/her business both reside in the same community?

3. **Incorporate next steps into the conversation.** Look for any opportunities to involve the prospect in any aspect of your organization: attending an event, completing a perception survey, drafting a testimonial to be featured in a giving brochure, speaking to a group of individuals served by your organization, etc.

Any involvement options will allow you to reconnect with the prospect.

End the conversation by agreeing to reconnect, e.g., "After you have had time to complete this brief survey, I'll schedule another appointment to get your feedback."

8 Encourage Area Civic Groups To Raise Funds on Your Behalf

Do you encourage your community's civic groups — Kiwanis, Rotary, etc. — to initiate fundraising projects on behalf of your organization?

You can establish an ongoing gift-revenue stream by having a procedure in place that encourages service clubs and other groups to take on your organization as one of their help projects. To do that:

1. Provide programs to area clubs that showcase the work of your organization. Then, as you conclude each talk, point out how the club can help your cause.

2. Get a directory of area clubs in your region, determine the elected leadership of each and then meet with the officers — or send a personalized letter with a bounce-back — that invites them to initiate a fundraising project with your organization named recipient of the funds they raise.

3. Look to your current donors and volunteers. Find out which organizations they belong to and then encourage them to serve as ambassadors on your behalf, convincing their clubs to initiate fundraising projects to benefit your organization.

9 Achieve 100 Percent Employee Giving on the First Try

In her first year as director of development and alumni affairs at Midway College (Midway, KY), Di Boyer helped achieve the first 100 percent participation rate for the faculty and staff campaign fund, with gifts averaging $250.

Boyer credits the campaign's success to a combination of setting the bar high and encouraging practical, yet creative campaign management.

After much discussion with her staff, Boyer says she realized one reason the staff campaign had never achieved 100 percent giving was simply because faculty and staff had never been challenged to do so. So her department's first step was to set 100 percent participation as a tangible goal.

The next decision was just as innovative: "We did not run the campaign out of the development office," she explains. "We specifically picked a campaign chair who was a faculty volunteer. Not only did this take the heat off the development office, whose time and talents were already overstretched, but it also forced them to throw out the old story. There would be no more walking around with pledge forms."

Charged with encouraging giving at a college located in the heart of horse country, the volunteer committee came up with the campaign theme, The Midway Meet. Each faculty and staff department was treated like one horse in a race, so it became a fun challenge for each department to try to cross the finish line ahead of the others.

As a thank-you for giving, all donors were taken to see Smarty Jones, the 2004 Kentucky Derby winner, at a nearby horse farm.

Midway College has kept up the 100 percent participation streak every year since, making only a few tweaks to the program.

The annual campaign now has two co-chairs — one from the faculty, the other from non-teaching staff to equally represent both constituencies. The co-chairs choose a theme. For the 2009 Thanks A Latte campaign, donors received McDonald's lattes and Midway coffee mugs and had their pictures taken with their mugs for their mug shots.

Source: Di Boyer, Director of Development and Alumni Affairs, Midway College, Midway, KY. Phone (859) 846-5485. E-mail: dboyer@midway.edu. Website: www.midway.edu

10 Don't Overlook Short-term Alumni as Prospects

Cyrus Nathan, son of a globe-trotting U.S. consul, spent just two years at Chestnut Hill Academy (Philadelphia, PA). But he never forgot the experience, and 80 years after his 1930 graduation, he left the school a bequest of $2.2 million.

While major donors are often four-year or K-12 alumni, development officials should not ignore persons who attend only a year or two, says Betsy Longstreth, director of institutional advancement. "They donate significant amounts more often than you might imagine," she says, noting that a recent gift of $700,000 came from an individual who spent just one year at Chestnut Hill.

"The most important thing is maintaining personal contact with your donors and being alert for signs of real connection to the school," she says. "Both of these donors provided years of steady support at a lower level, showing a sincere commitment over a lifetime. Those are the kinds of people you want to focus on, even if the gifts are not yet large."

Longstreth says advancement officials had no knowledge of Nathan's bequest until notified by his family. The gift endowed six faculty chairs while providing an important catalyst for a major fundraising campaign marking the school's 150th anniversary.

Source: Betsy Longstreth, Director of Institutional Advancement, Chestnut Hill Academy, Philadelphia, PA. Phone (215) 247-4700. E-mail: Blongstreth@chestnuthillacademy.org

11 Win New Friends By Seeking Their Input

Here's a great way to introduce your nonprofit to dozens of new prospects and, at the same time, accumulate information that will be helpful for future fundraising efforts.

Arrange interviews with 10 or more individuals who have little or no relationship with your organization to find out what they know or don't know about your organization.

Ask them questions such as:

✓ In your opinion, what is our organization known for?
✓ Who do we mostly serve?
✓ What services do we provide?
✓ What have you heard about our organization that's positive?
✓ What negative comments have you heard about our organization?
✓ Based on what you know about our organization, what should we be doing differently?
✓ When you think of all of the nonprofit organizations in our community, where would you rank ours in order of importance?
✓ Which organizations would you place at the top of your list based on importance?

Getting answers to questions such as these not only gives you valuable information on public perception, it also serves as a first step to involving new prospects in the life of your organization. You can use this procedure as a way to introduce yourself and your organization.

Use these initial meetings as a reason to go back to those having been surveyed to share with them how their input was used to make changes and improvements.

The raw material you receive may be used to help write marketing materials, produce a Q&A page on your website, make changes to programs or services or any number of other uses.

Use this information-seeking method to win new friends and learn from their perceptions.

12 Attract First-time Business Donors

Want to get more businesses giving to your charity? Begin by identifying a service or product they offer that could be contributed as a gift-in-kind. Businesses view gifts-in-kind as less costly, and they will serve to involve the business in your organization and begin a habit of giving that can lead to cash gifts.

13 Broaden Donor Base With Club Of Like-thinkers

If you have a handful of like-minded individuals already committed to your cause — retired teachers, 20-somethings, professional women, stay-at-home moms, CPAs or fans of a sports team — consider helping them form a club. In addition to helping them connect, make new friends and enjoy camaraderie, you can also encourage them to work as a team to take on a funding or other project for the benefit of your charity.

Let's say you have a dozen 20-somethings who support your cause individually. Invite them all to form a club that meets on a monthly basis. Together, come up with a funding project the group can take on as their own. In addition to making personal gifts toward the project, part of their aim would be to enlist more members.

If 50 club members each contributed $100 each year for five years, they will have funded a $25,000 project.

Use this same model to start other clubs made up of various affinity groups. Over time, you can build a large and diverse base of involved donors.

14 Raise First-time Gifts in a Down Economy

Looking for ways to generate first-time gifts in a down economy? You can do so, with a positive attitude and these strategies:

- Ask a loyal board member or major donor to establish a challenge gift that matches all new donors' gifts.

- Conduct a direct mail appeal to nondonors asking for small gifts for any of a handful of compelling funding projects.

- Kick off a special fundraising effort among existing loyal donors: "Recruit a new friend for..." Then hold a party at the end of the effort inviting everyone who rose to the occasion, along with your new donors.

- Coordinate a special event. Anyone attending who's not already a donor becomes a first-time contributor.

- Meet with corporate decision makers and convince them to coordinate an in-house campaign encouraging their employees to support a particular project that won't get accomplished without their support.

- Share a list of fundraising projects for local civic groups from which current and potential donors can choose.

- Launch a new membership program that includes special benefits for anyone who joins.

15 Look to Social Media to Expand Your Reach

Social media is one of the trendiest ways nonprofits can raise funds. But with your budget and staff already stretched, how can you implement social media into your efforts?

Take a cue from Big Brothers Big Sisters of America (BBBS), a Philadelphia, PA-based nonprofit that uses many social media venues. Here, Cheyenne Palma, director of development, shares what works for the organization:

Twitter is one of the largest online social networking sites, and it's easy to get lost in all the tweets. How do you use this site productively?

"We try to tweet once a day during the work week; and we only follow legitimate people who follow us; and we also follow up with a direct message to further engage new followers."

Facebook is another site that is seeing exponential growth. How does your Facebook fan page work for you?

"We have 4,035 fans, an increase of more than 40 percent for the year and our Facebook Causes site currently has 1,896 members who have donated $613. To keep the fan page current and reduce time spent on it, we simply integrated our RSS feed into the site. We've also learned much of our current donor base is active on Facebook and through research and data analysis, we have located nearly 20 percent of them on the site."

LinkedIn is known more for its corporate network and as a place for like-minded business people to connect. Do you feel nonprofit fundraising has a place on LinkedIn?

"We are still in the very early stages of determining how we will use LinkedIn. We've begun to identify board members and donors who are active on LinkedIn, but have yet to complete this analysis. We have discussed using the Events module and the Groups functionality to connect with specific donors and supporters on LinkedIn. We anticipate this will be a much more targeted effort and not as broad an approach as Facebook."

It seems that cell phones can do just about everything now, including depositing paychecks online. Will BBBS dip its toes in the mobile giving waters?

"We are now piloting the ability to donate funds via texting and have 11 agencies testing text giving. Primarily, we are testing its usage at local events, such as radiothons and baseball games. It appears there is potential where we have a very large, captive audience.

"We also anticipate folding mobile giving into our social media fundraising efforts through fundraising widgets. By placing a text-giving widget on select sites, viewers won't even need to go to a separate donation page to contribute, they can simply send a text."

What do you think is important for non-profits venturing into social media to remember? And if they're not already doing it, should they be?

"It's important for nonprofits to be involved in social media, particularly because it's the wave of the future. If you look at future generations of donors, it's how they communicate.

"An exaggerated example of this was demonstrated in a news article I read online recently about two teenage girls in Australia trapped in a storm drain — they updated their Facebook status instead of dialing for help! This is the future donor base that fundraisers are looking at tapping into; they need to get on board now, even if it's just to get their name and their message out there.

"Even from a budgetary perspective it makes sense: a few personnel hours per week can lead to donations that you might not otherwise have gotten, and there's no outside overhead to set it up or maintain it, if you do it all in-house."

Source: Cheyenne Palma, Director of Development, Big Brothers Big Sisters of America, Philadelphia, PA. Phone (215) 665-7765, E-mail: cheyenne.palma@bbbs.org

16 Use Satellite Locations to Strengthen Relationships

Does your organization have any type of off-site locations (branch campus, counseling offices, medical facility)? If you have locations other than your primary one, take advantage of those secondary sites to build relationships with would-be contributors.

Here are some ways to reach out to satellite locations and build relationships:

1. **Develop one or more advisory groups for each of the locations.** Involve people from those communities in meaningful ways. Ask for their input on issues. Train them to raise funds on behalf of your organization. Ask for their help in coordinating educational programs for the community.

2. **Plan a yearlong schedule of awareness-building activities.** Hold monthly events that bring key employees from your headquarters to the off-site locations. Schedule special-interest programs. Host receptions. Provide lectures or screenings.

3. **Bring others to your headquarters.** Host one or more special receptions or events at your primary facility for out-of-towners to attend. Consider scheduling a bus to bring in groups from each of your satellite locations.

17 Consider 'In Lieu Of' Gift Option

Persons who wish to support the Deborah Hospital Foundation (Browns Mills, NJ) have a unique way to do so: The In Lieu Of donation program. Ellen Krivchenia, director of national chapter services, explains:

How does the program work?

"People celebrating a special occasion such as a wedding, birthday or anniversary contact us to create personalized cards that either request guests donate to the hospital in lieu of purchasing a gift, or in the event of a wedding, the card might say that a donation has been made in the guests' names in lieu of them receiving party favors."

How do you make your program unique?

"My assistant handles the design aspect and works one-on-one with those making the requests to make sure they get exactly what they're looking for. From font to color palette, each one is unique."

Where/when do you promote the program?

"While we informally launched the program in 2008, we didn't promote it at all. But in January 2009, we started publicizing it on our website and through our print publication that goes out to our foundation members. Since then, we have had about 10 new clients with whom we've worked."

What is the average donation?

"We're averaging about $500 per event. I think as more people see our cards at events, the more interest we'll get, and I anticipate donations will increase over time."

Who is taking advantage of this program?

"Individuals who are looking for more meaningful ways to spend their money. If a bride and groom can make a donation to the hospital rather than buy bags of mints for their reception tables, they'll do it. It's the same with the couple celebrating their 50th wedding anniversary — they don't need anything, why not encourage guests to make a donation that can help save a life instead?"

Source: Ellen Krivchenia, Director of National Chapter Services, Deborah Hospital Foundation, Browns Mills, NJ. Phone (669)893-3372. E-mail: dhfnjro@deborahfoundation.org. Website: www.deborahfoundation.org

18 Publicity That Garners Gifts

Although publicity in and of itself won't bring in an avalanche of gifts — it takes a direct ask to do that — it can certainly plant "giving seeds" in the minds of those you hope to reach and nurture existing relationships.

Support your PR office's efforts by pointing out ways they can help fundraising efforts through awareness-building publicity:

✓ Features on the impact particular gifts are having on your organization and those you serve.

✓ Updates of giving to date in relation to goals and past giving.

✓ Stories on your organization's economic impact.

✓ Trends that reflect favorably on the need for your organization and its services.

✓ Announcements of realized bequests and other major gifts.

✓ Historical articles about your organization and its importance.

✓ News and features of particular accomplishments your organization has made.

✓ Announcements of board and volunteer appointments.

✓ Features on the clients you serve.

✓ Announcements of new sponsorships or partnerships.

✓ Editorials from board members, donors and friends lauding your organization's efforts.

✓ News and features about your employees' expertise, accomplishments and community involvement.

✓ News about the accomplishments of your current and former clients.

19 Offer Incentives to Participate in Letter-writing Campaign

What does nearly every college student need? Money. That was the motivation behind California State University (Long Beach, CA) offering $2,000 as the grand prize for attendees at the Up 'til Dawn fundraising event for St. Jude Children's Research Hospital.

To be eligible for the prize, attendees had to address at least 75 quality envelopes to family and friends with pre-written letters enclosed asking for donations to the hospital. The winner was chosen randomly and received a check for $2,000.

Courtney Day, executive director of the event, says they learned the hard way that requiring participants to use quality addresses was key.

"Many people wanted to write 75 letters but didn't have that many addresses, so they would make up fake ones," Day says. "Every fake letter actually costs the hospital $1."

Part of the prize money came as an award from Wells Fargo. Day says that when they received it, it made sense to use it as an incentive for the letter-writing campaign. "It was a great way to spend it, because it would give back to our campus, which seemed fair because we asked them to give to the community of St. Jude."

Day says the incentive has proven successful, increasing the number of quality letters sent from 4,000 to 6,000 in just one year. The letter-writing campaign has raised more than $80,000 for the hospital since its inception at Long Beach in 2005.

Source: Courtney Day, Executive Director, Up 'til Dawn, California State University at Long Beach, Long Beach, CA. Phone (562) 243-2069. E-mail: c.day88@yahoo.com

20 Do Pet Memorials Make Sense for Your Organization?

Pet memorials: Humane societies do it. And with the ever-increasing popularity of pets and growing number of people who consider their pets as important members of their families, even some other types of nonprofit organizations are beginning to do it.

Could your organization justify inviting memorial gifts in memory of a beloved pet?

If you can start with a few individuals who choose to do this, publicize their acts of love in your honor roll of contributors and elsewhere to encourage others to do the same. Over time, you may be pleasantly surprised by the number of people who are drawn to make a contribution in memory (or in honor) of their pets.

21 Chalk Up $25,000 in New Gifts From Businesses

Whether you are after $25,000 or $250,000, it's important to establish and stick to a fundraising plan. To secure $25,000 in new gift revenue from area businesses, consider these steps:

1. Ask a board member or existing business donor to establish a challenge gift that will match all new and increased gifts from businesses for the next three years.

2. Pull together a group of 25 volunteers who are already committed to and contributing to your organization.

3. Ask each volunteer to help you raise $1,000 in new or increased gifts from the business community during the next 12 months. Then meet with them on a monthly basis to review progress, discuss prospect names and make new assignments.

4. Establish a club or program with benefits aimed at businesses that give at a certain level, making it hard for businesses to say "no" to volunteers' invitations to join.

22 Explore Unique Sponsorship Possibilities

Could you be missing out on sponsorship opportunities that might appeal to particular types of businesses, even individuals? Spend time brainstorming with staff and other employees to identify particular programs or departments that could be underwritten with sponsorships.

To help get your wheels turning, ask yourself if any of these sponsorship ideas might have potential at your nonprofit:

- Get someone to underwrite the cost of vehicles (purchase and/or maintenance) used to help those you serve. Sponsor signs could even be placed on vans and other vehicles.

- Secure a business to sponsor your entire annual fund or membership drive for the year. Tie the sponsor's name to your annual fund theme, your campaign kickoff, brochures and other associated components.

- Line up businesses to sponsor groups of those you serve. If you represent a school, for example, groups of businesses could sponsor particular classes. If you represent a hospital, businesses could sponsor certain care units (e.g., oncology, neonatal, cardiology, etc.).

23   Heritage Circle Giving Society Focuses on $1,000-plus Donors

Staff with the Wisconsin Historical Foundation (Madison, WI) — the official fundraising and gift-receiving organization for the Wisconsin Historical Society — are focusing on increasing the number of members in its $1,000-plus-a-year Heritage Circle level.

"We've added benefits for members at this level including invitations to exclusive events and activities, complimentary gift VIP parking privileges, and special recognition in our Honor Roll of Donors and Members in addition to the regular benefits of society membership," says Jeanne L. Engle, the foundation's director of development.

Between July 1, 2009, (the start of the Wisconsin Historical Foundation's fiscal year) and Jan. 5, 2010, some 64 donors had made commitments for unrestricted gifts of $1,000 or more, qualifying them for membership in The Heritage Circle. This was up from 49 such donors during the same time in the previous fiscal, says Martha Truby, associate director of annual giving.

Organizers developed a special package for soliciting prospective members from The Heritage Circle level that includes:

- A letter inviting prospective donors to join The Heritage Circle (to which a development staff member or officer usually adds a handwritten note).
- A Heritage Circle brochure — a tri-fold with a pocket into which a list of Heritage Circle donors and a list of Heritage Circle benefits is inserted.
- A customized reply device.

"As we qualify donors who have been identified with having higher financial capacity, we make a personal appeal for membership in The Heritage Circle," says Engle. These personal appeals may be a letter with a handwritten note, a face-to-face visit or a phone call.

To build awareness for The Heritage Circle, they branded it separately with a special logo embedded with the tag line: Leading the Way.

"We created a separate logo because we wanted to reinforce the message that membership in the Heritage Circle means being part of something special," says Truby. "Our goal is to engage them with small group cultivation events, behind-the-scenes tours and insider information. Savvy investors are passionate about our mission, and we want them to understand the impact they have on our organization by offering them opportunities to become engaged in what we do."

One new benefit is allowing members to choose their own complimentary gift, says Truby. They can choose one of four books produced by the Wisconsin Historical Society Press, or one of four prints reproduced from the society's extensive image collection. "This is offered with a coupon that is sent with their Heritage Circle member packet," she says. "Several recipients of the coupon added a thank-you note saying they really appreciated the gift."

A key to their early success in attracting Heritage Circle members has been a commitment by development officers to view annual gifts of equal importance as one-time major gifts, says Truby. "Annual gifts help develop a habit of giving that sometimes one large donation can't do."

Sources: Jeanne L. Engle, Director of Development; Martha Truby, Associate Director of Annual Giving, Wisconsin Historical Foundation, Madison, WI. Phone (608) 264-6580 (Engle); (608) 261-9363 (Truby) E-mail: jeanne.engle@wisconsinhistory.org; martha.truby@wisconsinhistory.org

Content not available in this edition

Promotional Materials Encourage New $1,000 Donors

Materials promoting the $1,000 giving level, The Heritage Circle, of the Wisconsin Historical Foundation (Madison, WI) include brochures listing member benefits, right, and a letter of invitation that features the following wording:

By joining the Heritage Circle, you will enable the Wisconsin Historical Society to:

- *Safeguard our most precious historical treasures.*
- *Preserve the Wisconsin Historic Sites experience.*
- *Transform how Wisconsin history is taught and learned.*
- *Share local history and support Wisconsin's communities.*

24 Cultivate New Parents, Grandparents

The birth of a baby is an extraordinary experience. Why not have your organization be a part of it by congratulating the new parents and grandparents with a personal note and a gift that's uniquely yours?

Some nonprofits will direct a keepsake letter to the newborn, welcoming him/her into the world. Others will send the parents an inexpensive gift that includes their logo.

Whatever you choose to do, don't miss sharing in the joy of this special occasion.

25 Annual Giving Strategies: Offer Restricted Gifts

Although the pressure is on to raise more unrestricted gifts during tough economic times, you may actually have greater success marketing restricted gifts — those that fund specific programs or projects.

Why?

Because would-be contributors are more likely to support those funding projects that interest them. They don't want to think their gifts are going into some big black hole.

In addition to soliciting unrestricted gifts supporting general operations (e.g., scholarships, patient care, client services), carry out targeted asks that include restricted gift options.

You may share a wish list of restricted gift opportunities with nondonors, for example. Or later in your fiscal year you may ask those who have already made an unrestricted gift to consider a second gift restricted to a project of their choosing.

26 Ask New Prospects for a Gift They Can't Refuse

You wouldn't ask every first-time donor for a mere $25 gift in a face-to-face call, but there are times when a modest request is the way to go. Here's an example of such a scenario which, while it shouldn't be used in all instances, can secure that first-time gift with the intent of building a habit — and increased levels of giving — over time:

Prospect: "I'm sorry, but I'm really not interested in making a gift to your organization at this time."

Development Officer: "I realize that you're not all that familiar with our programs and services, but I'm frankly only here today to ask for a mere $25 gift. One of our board members has agreed to match all new $25 gifts up to $2,500. That's 100 gifts we're hoping to generate within the next 60 days to, in effect, double the amount we will benefit. Can we count on you for a $25 gift?"

Prospect: "Well, when you put it that way, how can I refuse?"

27 Help Set Introductory Appointments

Most veteran development professionals will agree that making cold calls is an uphill battle. Setting an appointment can, in itself, be a nearly impossible task — unless you have the right person doing it for you.

Enlist the help of your organization's current friends and supporters, your centers of influence, to help gain entry into the homes and offices of new prospects, especially those capable of making generous annual gifts.

To help centers of influence help you, develop an introductory letter they can use as a template in developing letters of their own. The letter can be used by these willing volunteers as a first step in setting an appointment with new prospects, friends and associates of theirs who might be willing to contribute to your cause. Providing these volunteers with a sample introductory letter will take the guesswork away and show them how easy it is for them to help gain access to their friends and associates.

Encourage willing centers of influence to use their own letterhead (if possible) when sending these appointment-setting letters.

> Dear [Name]:
>
> I have been a longtime contributor to The Raskin Museum for several reasons:
>
> ✓ Raskin holds an important place in our community's and our state's history.
>
> ✓ The Raskin Museum provides cultural opportunities that enhance the quality of life in the surrounding region.
>
> ✓ The museum continues to give future generations a greater sense of pride in our region's heritage.
>
> This important community asset would not exist were it not for the generosity of many individuals and businesses. And I know first hand of some of the exciting plans that are in the works for the months and years ahead.
>
> [Name], I would be very grateful if you would allow Mark Heistercamp and me to meet with you briefly sometime during the next couple of weeks to tell you more about the museum and share some of the exciting plans that are in store for the months ahead. I promise we'll take no more than a half hour of your time.
>
> I'll give you a call in a few days to set up a time and day that works best for you.
>
> Thanks in advance, [Name], for your willingness to meet with us.
>
> Yours truly,
>
> Jim Thompson

28 Seven Ways to Promote Your Brick Campaign

Engraved brick campaigns are a great way to raise money for a specific project or program while beautifying an outdoor area. Here are seven ways to promote your brick campaign:

1. Include the campaign brochure in gift acknowledgments to donors who give to your annual fund or other programs.

2. Create a website specifically for promoting the brick campaign. Include information about where the money raised will go, how to purchase a brick, criteria for wording on the bricks, a map of where the bricks will be located, etc.

3. Send an e-mail solicitation to constituents for whom you have e-mail addresses, directing them to the brick campaign website for more information or to purchase a brick.

4. Create a traveling display for your brick campaign for external events, speaking engagements, etc.

5. Place ads about the campaign in your organization's newsletter, special donor publications and magazine.

6. Send a targeted mailing to memorial donors.

7. At the brick site, place a tasteful marker or notice stating the purpose of the engraved bricks and whom to contact to purchase a brick.

29 OMG! Agency Raising Funds Via Text Messaging

On Oct. 24, 2009, Louisiana State University (LSU) of Baton Rouge, LA, played Auburn University (Auburn, AL) in football at LSU's Tiger Stadium, but the real winner was Capital Area United Way (Baton Rouge, LA).

That's the day United Way staff and supporters took a leadership role in the move to incorporate mobile technology into fundraising efforts by capturing donations by text message.

To do so, the organization teamed up with mGive.com (a service of Mobile Accord, Denver, CO); Diane Allen & Associates Advertising & Public Relations, Inc. (Baton Rouge, LA); and LSU Athletics, giving donors the opportunity to instantly react to a fundraising appeal and confirm their donation by sending a text.

During the football game, LSU used game announcements and a Jumbotron ad to ask the 90,000 attendees to each donate $5 to Capital Area United Way by texting the letters "LSU" to 864833. Donations were charged to texters' monthly cell phone bills and identified as a nontaxable donation.

"An event on this scale has never been attempted before, and could mark a new era in fundraising," says Karen Profita, president/CEO of the United Way chapter. "We generated an amazing buzz with this effort. It was great to see the supportive fans united to help the community."

The event brought in $8,550 with more than 2,558 text messages sent. More than 800 people did not confirm the required second step in the text message donation process, so Profita asked fans to go back and ensure they confirmed. This resulted in an additional $465 in donations, bringing the total to $9,015.

Source: Karen Profita, President/CEO, Capital Area United Way, Baton Rouge, LA. Phone (225) 346-5817. E-mail: karenp@cauw.org. Website: www.cauw.org/content/ways_to_give

30 Direct a Newsletter to Sponsors, Would-be Sponsors

To convince more businesses to support your organization and encourage existing donors to give at higher levels, consider pursuing sponsorships rather than outright gifts.

To cultivate new and increased sponsorships, consider a monthly or quarterly newsletter directed to existing and would-be sponsors. To keep costs in line, you might want to make it an e-newsletter.

What might such a sponsors' newsletter include in the way of content? Here's a sampling of the possibilities:

- New or enhanced sponsorship benefits.
- Profiles of current sponsors and what they are underwriting.
- Recognition of newly enlisted sponsors.
- Brief descriptions of sponsorship opportunities.
- Features about how a particular sponsorship is impacting your organization's programs and services.
- A regular message from the chair of your sponsorship advisory council.
- Announcements of upcoming sponsors-only events.
- Messages from those who are benefiting from sponsorship support.
- A calendar of upcoming events for your organization that spotlights sponsor-funded or supported happenings.
- A request to forward the e-newsletter to others in their circle of influence.

31 Make a Personal Phone Call to All First-time Donors

Making new donors feel appreciated can lead them to be longtime donors.

Erica Hart, assistant director of scholarships and annual giving at Georgia Perimeter College (Decatur, GA), says she calls all new donors (except corporate and foundation donors) within three days of the receipt of their gift. She doesn't use a script, but simply introduces herself and says, "I wanted to thank you for your recent gift in support of (area the gift supports)." She tells them about the program and asks them to update their information. If no one answers she leaves the information in a voice mail.

"I check the year they graduated, their major, what teachers they were involved with, and ask them about their memories of the college," she says. "They are more than willing to talk because it's not a solicitation call. Most donors are surprised by the call. Some say, 'It was only a small gift,' or 'I know it's not much.' Many say 'Thank you for calling me.' Sometimes they have questions. If I can't answer them, I will pass the question on to someone who can and then follow up to make sure it was answered."

The information she collects is passed on to the alumni department. Persons who give more than $1,000 are also contacted by the director of institutional advancement by phone or letter, says Hart.

Source: Erica Hart, Assistant Director of Scholarships and Annual Giving at Georgia Perimeter College, Decatur, GA. Phone (678) 891-2559. E-mail: Erica.Hart@gpc.edu

32 Explore In-kind Gifts With Nondonors

Getting someone to make that first contribution — especially someone with no direct ties to your nonprofit — can be challenging. That's why you should consider an in-kind contribution as a first-time connecting point.

In addition to tangible in-kind gifts (e.g., vehicles, office furniture, supplies, equipment), look for pro bono services that may not be obvious at first glance. Weigh various aspects of what a business does, or look at the professional expertise of individuals: What services do they perform that would be of benefit to your cause? What expertise do they possess that your nonprofit could use?

Nondonors are often more prepared to share a product or service than cash. Building loyalty with in-kind gifts will more than likely result in cash gifts down the road.

33 Give Tours That Invite Support

If you do not currently give donors and would-be donors tours of your facilities, consider doing so. Familiarity with your organization leads to involvement; involvement leads to ownership; and ownership results in gifts, large and small.

If you offer tours, analyze whether you are using them to maximize the likelihood of receiving financial support.

To make your tours more profitable:

- Let the public know through all available means that you offer and welcome regular tours of your facilities.

- Train tour guides (staff or volunteers) to recognize giving potential.

- Throughout the tour, have the guides point out projects that could be realized if sufficient funding was in place.

- Make sure named rooms and buildings are properly marked. Have guides point out recognition plaques and mention donors by name.

- Give guests a look at your organization at work. For a college or university, peek into a student-filled classroom. For a youth organization, visit with some young people.

- As you walk between points of interest, interject key messages that point out gift opportunities: "Our endowment is beginning to grow thanks to the generosity of some who have remembered the institution in their estate plans."

- Share messages that demonstrate confidence in your organization's future: "Our plans call for expanding the neonatal department soon, based on the growing needs of this region."

- If guests exhibit more interest in a particular area, slow down and allow them to learn more; you may have just discovered their funding interests.

- Take a few minutes at tour's end to sit in an office or conference room and summarize key points or programs and seek guest feedback. Again, you may unearth their areas of interest.

- Send them on their way with appropriate literature and a memento of their visit. Then, send a follow-up note telling them what a pleasure it was to show them your facilities.

Your thoughtful planning and execution of facility tours will serve as a viable strategy for generating additional gift income.

34 Five Ways to Generate an Extra $10,000

Maybe your annual fund goal was increased by $10,000 this year or perhaps the absence of past gifts has left a $10,000 hole in what needs to be generated. In either case, here are five ways to pick up an extra $10,000 in annual gift revenue:

1. Pull together a group of experienced volunteers to develop a special event aimed at reaching new donors.
2. Make 50 personal calls to new prospects capable of making $1,000 gifts. That's a 1-5 ratio needed to generate 10 gifts of $1,000.
3. Organize a group of existing donors willing to help launch a 30-day campaign aimed at nondonor members of the business community.
4. Get someone to establish a $5,000 challenge gift that will match all new and increased gifts for the year.
5. Plan a series of direct mail appeals, each intended to fund a different project and direct each appeal to a different group.

35 Offer Variety of Auction Styles to Boost Results

How does the GAMBIT Auction and Dinner of Canisius High School (Buffalo, NY) raise around $300,000 every year? Its 36-year history helps, but so does offering a variety of auction events, says Colleen Sellick, GAMBIT program coordinator.

The fundraiser begins months before the night of the event as parents and alumni hold up to a dozen parties to gather the 500 to 600 auction items every year. This extended season raises awareness for the auction and allows a wide range of supporters to become involved, says Sellick.

At the event, most gifts are distributed via silent auction. Items with bid sheets attached are displayed in five large groups that are progressively closed as the night proceeds. Larger items are reserved for the final group, and a grand finale offers a last chance at anything still available.

Following the silent auction, a live auction showcases two dozen of the most valuable and unusual gifts. Real-time action helps drive bids higher, says Sellick, and limiting the number of items offered helps retain interest and attention.

A gift website complements the traditional auction catalog as it displays all auction items and sorts them into categories to make navigation easier while allowing development staff to analyze the yield from different kinds of gifts and advise prospective donors accordingly. (Sellick says electronics, sports memorabilia, unique items and vacation homes generally offer great returns for their price.)

The school also began auctioning items directly online this year using the online Web service Maestrosoft (www.maestrosoft.com). So far Sellick has simply sold the items outright, but notes that another option involves using the highest online bid as the starting bid for on-site live or silent auctions.

While the online component is in trial stages, Sellick has already seen benefits. "We have received donations and bids from around the country," she says. "In the future, this will be a great way to reach beyond our immediate community. And for now, just getting the word out about this feature has driven people to the website and increased our direct online donations, which is a great start!"

Source: Colleen Sellick, GAMBIT Coordinator, Canisius High School, Buffalo, NY. Phone (716) 882-0466. E-mail: Sellick@canisiushigh.org

36 Three Changes To Boost Your Annual Appeal

Looking to pump up results for your annual appeal? So were officials at Lawrence University (Appleton, WI). And they're finding success doing so with three simple changes, says Ben Campbell, associate director of annual giving.

Campbell shares the three techniques they have recently added to breathe new life into their annual fundraising program:

- **Communicate via e-mail.** Campbell says he is testing a new idea with a small number of class agents where they send out an e-mail to their classmates, in addition to the regular letters and calls they make. He says agents are encouraged to make the e-mail positive and personal, while sharing some numbers about the current state of the campaign.
- **Send an early-bird mailing.** Sent at the beginning of the next fiscal year, this encourages giving early and gives a jump-start to your campaign. In Lawrence University's case, Campbell says, this mailing grabs people's attention because of its unexpected timing.
- **Switch appeal order.** Campbell says they have five main direct mail appeals each year. Two of them are class agent mailings. These used to be the second and third appeals, but are now the second (behind only the new early-bird mailing) and fifth to maximize the opportunity to receive gifts early in the fiscal year and act as a catch-all at the end.

Source: Benjamin C. Campbell, Associate Director of Annual Giving, Lawrence University, Appleton, WI. Phone (920) 832-6936. E-mail: benjamin.c.campbell@ lawrence.edu

37 Host a Tour of Nonprofits

You're familiar with the traditional tour-of-homes fundraiser that many organizations host each year. Why not get together with other nonprofits in your community and host a tour of community agencies?

Plan the event as a fund raiser with participating organizations splitting the proceeds, or simply use the opportunity to attract visitors to your collective facilities for a consciousness-raising tour of your programs and services — a way to attract future contributions and volunteers.

Whatever your objective, the event will require drawing-card appeal to motivate people to attend. Need some ideas?

- Call on interior designers, retailers and greenhouses to decorate participating facilities for a week-long tour.
- Arrange to have respected community leaders or a noted celebrity at each of the agencies to meet and greet those who pay a visit.
- Conduct a progressive scavenger hunt. Those participating in agency tours — and securing clues at each stop — will have their names entered into a drawing for some wonderful donated prizes.
- Conduct a progressive chocolate-tasting extravaganza with mouth-watering delicacies at each stop.

It's a proven fact that people are much more likely to purchase a piece of clothing, if they first try it on. It's like that with worthwhile causes: People will be more inclined to become involved and/or contribute, if they become familiar with your mission and programs.

38 Educate All Employees About Fund Development

Your organization's employees can all play a role in various aspects of fund development, if you take the time to educate them on a regular basis. Here are some ways to do that:

1. Hold quarterly workshops for all employees and cover topics that can help them know how to identify, cultivate, steward and even solicit prospects.
2. Keep employees informed of your shop's activities and fundraising efforts through your in-house newsletter and e-mails.
3. Consider inexpensive incentives that reward employees who assist your efforts in various ways — citing them in in-house communications, and hosting a year-end employee recognition event.
4. Regularly invite employees to assist in particular development efforts — helping at special events, being present at functions in which donors and prospects are present, and participating in phonathons.

39 Challenge Gift Helps Leverage Phonathon Pledges

Looking for ways to improve your phonathon's results? Secure a challenge gift that callers can include in their pitch.

A challenge gift that will match all new and increased gifts not only helps to leverage giving, it energizes callers as well.

Here's an example of how a challenge gift might be incorporated into a caller's script:

Caller: "I have exciting news to share! One of our agency's board members has established a $50,000 challenge this year. The board member will match, dollar for dollar, any first-time gifts or any increases over last year up to $500 per donor.

"According to our records, Bill, you gave $100 last fiscal year. That means our challenger will match any increase you make up to $600 this year. Could you give $600 this year, Bill?"

Even if the person being contacted doesn't give the full ask amount, chances are they will respond to the challenge by making a first-time gift or contributing more than the previous year.

40 Create Some Friendly Competition Among Board Members

Want to get your board more actively involved in fund development? Create a friendly competition to see who can make the most asks or raise the most in gifts.

Try it for a four-month period to test its effectiveness.

Pair up board members, so they can make calls together, which is more fun than flying solo. Then divide the pairs into two teams. Give awards to the pair that achieves the best results and an award to the overall winning team as well.

Awards need not be expensive. Think of what would most motivate board members: a dinner prepared by your CEO, a gift certificate to a great restaurant, having one of your programs named in their honor for one year or whatever strikes their fancy.

The ultimate goal is to get your board members more involved with and energized by raising funds.

41 Six Ways to Build Your Mailing List

Building your mailing list is one obvious way to increase the number of annual contributors. To add qualified names to your database:

1. Place return postcards in your printed materials that say, "Please add my name to your mailing list."

2. Conduct drawings at special events and exhibits to gather names of attendees.

3. Include a guest book in your main lobby area.

4. Include an invitation on your website to receive information about your organization's news and upcoming events.

5. Invite donors, "customers" and your employees to share names of would-be donors.

6. Collect key lists of names to add to your database: contributors to other nonprofits, members of civic organizations, chamber of commerce members and more.

42 Birthday Club Builds Habits of Philanthropy

Imagine if one child's birthday could help other children celebrate more of their own. That's the impact of the Birthday Club at Huntsville Hospital Foundation (Huntsville, AL), as children ask persons to make donations to the foundation in lieu of birthday gifts.

The foundation created the club in 2008 to introduce the concepts of giving and sharing to children, according to Anna Roberson, manager of community events. "Our hope is that philanthropy will become such a part of their lives that they will become active volunteers and donors as adults," Roberson says.

Here's how the program works:

A parent whose child would like to celebrate a birthday in this way contacts foundation staff, who assist the parent in creating a Birthday Club website page, including a special message from the birthday child and, if appropriate, stating the specific hospital department or need the gifts will fund. The foundation provides guests with inserts to include in birthday party invitations, providing instructions on how to donate or shop online.

The birthday child requests that monetary donations be brought to the party or guests shop for designated items on the foundation's website, with parents paying with a credit card and foundation staff arranging for the items to be purchased for the chosen department.

Roberson says the parents of the birthday children have been pleased with the program, and eager to share the importance of giving back with their children. This connection has also extended to the parents of the party guests, allowing the foundation to develop relationships with them, many of whom have gone on to become foundation donors themselves.

And while the return may be small — most birthday parties average around $100 in donations, with the program raising nearly $10,000 since its inception — Roberson says the effort is worthwhile. "The biggest pro is the spirit of philanthropy demonstrated by the youngest members of our community. Even the smallest gift gives us an opportunity to say thanks, and later cultivate donors for larger gifts."

Source: Anna Roberson, Manager of Community Events, Huntsville Hospital Foundation, Huntsville, AL. Phone (256) 265-9461. E-mail: annaroberson@hhsys.org

43 Social Media Offers New Twist On Old Campaign

The health insurance company CDPHP (Albany, NY) has long been a supporter of the Regional Food Bank of Northeastern New York (Latham, NY).

One way CDPHP staff show support for the food bank is with the CDPHP Holiday appeal, in which the company donates $5,000, and then pledges to match donations of $100 or more from other companies up to an additional $5,000.

In honor of the tenth anniversary of the appeal and in recognition of the increasing importance of social media in promotions and fundraising, CDPHP partners decided to add a new twist: matching donations of $100 or more up to $5,000, and donating $5 for every new "like" on the food bank's Facebook account up to an additional $5,000.

The switch helped raise more than $5,000 in addition to the $10,000 donation from CDPHP, says Mark Quandt, food bank executive director. Quandt adds that the food bank's Facebook friend numbers are growing fairly quickly, too, largely due to the CDPHP appeal.

The campaign has been widely promoted through local media coverage, area newspaper ads, billboard exposure, mail solicitations of CDPHP's vendors and prior food bank donors, and an e-newsletter sent to 2,500 food bank supporters.

Source: Mark Quandt, Executive Director, Regional Food Bank of Northeastern New York, Latham, NY. Phone (518) 786-3691. E-mail: markq@regionalfoodbank.net

Gift Club Tips

To give each of your gift clubs the attention it deserves, appoint a committee to each club and charge them with the responsibility for recruiting, retaining and recognizing donors at that level.

Turn to a Backup Plan When Annual Goal Is in Doubt

As you prepare your annual fundraising operational plan, map out a backup plan with fundraising strategies you can implement immediately should the possibility of reaching your yearly goal become questionable.

If, for instance, your fiscal year began in July and in January you find that you're shy of where you need to be, put that backup plan in place.

What strategies could your backup plan include? Although strategic elements will vary greatly from organization to organization, some examples include:

✓ Announcing a compelling mid-year funding project that will draw support from both existing donors and those persons who have yet to support your annual effort.

✓ Coordinating a fresh special event that was not a part of your original operational plan.

✓ Enlisting board members and others to call on lybunts and sybunts — those who gave last year, (or in some years), but not this year.

✓ Convincing a donor to establish a mid-year challenge gift that will match all new and increased gifts for the remainder of your fiscal year.

✓ Approaching businesses to sponsor particular programs or events as opposed to asking for outright gifts.

Use Commemorative Gifts to Reach New Donors

Since nondonors are more likely to donate toward something special, look for celebratory opportunities to invite support: your nonprofit's 10th, 25th or 50th anniversary, the retirement of your longtime CEO; and so forth.

If you're celebrating an anniversary, for instance, invite gifts of $1 for each year your organization has been in existence, and direct those gifts toward a funding project that would appeal to first-time donors.

Choosing a funding project that attracts the community's attention and makes people feel good about giving (e.g., a healing garden or indoor aviary for the enjoyment of those persons you serve) can boost your chances of attracting fresh support.

Raffles Prove Recession-proof for Fundraising

While creativity is a good thing, sometimes sticking with a proven event is better.

A prime example of this is the raffle. During a recession, a raffle accomplishes many things that bigger fundraisers usually can't. For instance, because people can get involved in a raffle for a relatively low cost, it can be a great way to attract first-time donors and increase your database.

Raffles also have staying power and can be held again and again, since for each one, the donor is not being asked to give much money or donate any time. People also like the nostalgic feel of raffles, especially during tough times. And from the perspective of development staff, raffles are practically free and very easy to operate.

The Appalachia Mission of Hope (McKee, KY), a Christian charitable organization, holds 12 or more successful raffles throughout the year. Even though the organization is located in an impoverished area, organizers say the raffles are a hit because ticket prices are set at only $1 per ticket, and because the prizes are always useful and enjoyable.

Ann Williams, director of operations, schedules raffles with holidays year-round, when people are more willing to spend a little extra in the hopes of having something nice for the holidays in return.

"In November, we raffle a huge basket of food items and gift certificate for a turkey or a Thanksgiving meal," Williams says. "For Easter, we raffle a basket stuffed with toys and goodies for a child. For Mother's Day and Father's Day, we raffle a basket of items for a lady and a basket of items for a man. In summer, we raffle a two-night stay at a motel coupled with tickets to some type of entertainment. We live some two-and-a-half hours from resort areas like Pigeon Forge and Gatlinburg, TN, so these locales work well for us."

Even without holiday themes, the mission has ongoing success raffling off dinner-and-a-movie packages. For a recent raffle, Williams collected gift certificates from seven restaurants and packaged them together into one raffle, she called Food for a Week.

One more mission-friendly trick about raffles. They are an easy way to foster one-on-one relationships within the community. Williams prefers to sell raffle tickets at the mission's small thrift store, where volunteers can make face-to-face contact with members of the community.

Source: Ann Williams, Director of Operations, Appalachia Mission of Hope, McKee, KY. Phone (606) 965-2449. E-mail: awilliams@amohonline.org

48

Enlist 100 Businesses At $100 Each

If your organization has little history of fund raising, it's important to begin to build a broad base of support that, hopefully, turns into repeat giving. One yearlong strategy is to enlist 100 business contributors who each give $100 (or more) with the expectation that they will begin contributing annually. (The number of businesses and dollar goal may differ depending on your community's size and the philanthropic environment.)

To implement this "100 business donors at $100 each" strategy:

1. Enlist a group of current business supporters who will agree to call on businesses on your behalf.
2. Develop a packet of materials volunteers (and you) can use to market $100-plus annual gifts.
3. Hold a series of small-group receptions at your facility or elsewhere as a means of telling your story to business attendees.
4. Coordinate a special event — golf classics are common examples — aimed at the business community with an entry fee of $100.
5. Conduct a phonathon on businesses using a funding project appealing to them.
6. Carry out at least two direct mail appeals during the year aimed at members of the business community.

49

7 Ways to Expand Your Prospect Database

Want to find new prospects to add to your mailing list? Try these ideas:

1. **Research.** Understand and use your mission to find clubs, associations and people who share the same interests as your organization.
2. **Follow the media.** Watch local news programs and subscribe to local publications to get the latest on new companies, business people, affluent members of the community, etc. Find out who they are, where they're from and their interests.
3. **Go public.** Go to local churches, clubs and giving circles and speak about your work. Send press releases or call newspaper editors when you have a newsworthy occasion, so that they might write about it.
4. **Create web presence.** Build your web page titles based on phrases for which you want to be found in search engines (e.g., Google). Include a newsletter or information sign-up option on your website or have people register to enter your site by entering their name and e-mail address.
5. **Recognize.** Talk to long-time supporters about the need to bring new donors to the organization. Offer recognition in publications and at special events for donors who bring in new donors. Add categories such as Agency Heroes or Agency Superstars to your existing donor categories for those who bring in new supporters.
6. **Keep your ears open.** Any time you hear someone in the community expressing interest in your organization, introduce yourself and ask for their business card, and if you can, put them on your mailing list.
7. **Utilize special events.** Have information request cards and sign-in forms at your events, so those interested can fill in their information. Offer some premium if they turn in a card or sign up (e.g., pens or refrigerator magnets with your organization's logo).

50

Exercise Every Opportunity To Convert Nondonors

Before eliminating nondonors' names from your mailing list, exhaust every option to convince them to give. There may be any number of reasons why they have not yet contributed — timing, who's doing the asking, how the funds will be used, lack of knowledge of an existing need, etc.

Follow strategies such as these to broaden your base of support and enlarge your pool of future major gift prospects:

- Create a wish list of specific, affordable funding options to trigger gifts.

- Convince someone to establish a challenge gift that matches all new gifts.

- Have volunteers review your list of nondonors for names they may know and have positive influence over.

- Offer a limited-time benefit or incentive to get new donors on board.

- Initiate a recruit-a-new-contributor campaign with volunteer help.

- Publicize contributors to date to encourage nondonors to be included.

- Insist that staff call on a minimum number of nondonors each month.

- Initiate a 5 percent campaign to increase overall donor participation by that amount while boosting awareness.

- Implement a phonathon directed only at nondonors on your mailing list.

51   Partner With Chamber of Commerce to Reach Businesses

In 2009, the Issaquah Schools Foundation (Issaquah, WA) entered into a fundraising/awareness-raising partnership with the local chamber of commerce that raises money while uniting the community around the common cause of education, says Robin Callahan, executive director of the Issaquah Schools Foundation. Callahan answers questions about the partnership:

How did the partnership come about?

"We received feedback about our previous business partnership campaign that the entry point for recognition, $1,500, was too much for local businesses. They wanted to commit, but couldn't always afford that kind of gift. So we began talking to our chamber of commerce about how the vitality of our community is dependent on the success of our schools. Together, we thought of ways the chamber could raise awareness about community involvement strengthening the district."

How does the program work?

"Local businesses can contribute at different levels, for different levels of recognition, which they choose from a menu of support (see below). The lowest level, $50 gift, gives you a cling-sticker for the window of your business, touting your business as a 'Business Partner — Proud to Invest in Great Schools and Great Communities.' It goes up from there."

How do you advertise your program?

"It happened that a local periodical had an entire issue of the magazine about how great schools make great communities, including a piece from the executive director of the chamber, and another from the superintendent of schools, and how strong schools promote vital and healthy community. So that summer, I sat down to write a letter with the chamber to be sent to all business members of the chamber, and we called upon that information to raise awareness for the foundation."

Source: Robin Callahan, Executive Director, Issaquah Schools Foundation, Issaquah, WA.
Phone (425) 416-2045. E-mail: rcallahan@issaquahschoolsfoundation.org.
Website: www.issaquahschoolsfoundation.org

Partnership Raises Funds, Awareness

A year-old partnership with the local chamber of commerce is beginning to pay off for the Issaquah Schools Foundation (Issaquah, WA), says Robin Callahan, the foundation's executive director:

"We've raised $2,500 to date, which covers our cost, but the initial benefit is that we've raised our participation level significantly: 40 businesses have responded (out of 400), which is 40 new business partners that we didn't have before.

"The feedback we've been getting has been positive: Business owners say they appreciate being able to support their schools; that they didn't know the foundation was out there; and they didn't know there was a need. This is the most promising element: We are spreading our message. We will be doing it again next year."

Content not available in this edition

52 Virtual Walkers Extend Event Reach

Your fundraising walk is a big day. But it's just one day — and what about the hundreds of people who can't make it on that day? Or the ones who could have made the date, but live too far away?

Virtual walkers are the answer, says Jennifer Matrazzo, associate executive director of Prevent Child Abuse New York (PCANY), Albany, NY. "Virtual walkers can still raise money towards the event without having to actually be there," Matrazzo says. "The idea is really just another way to expand the scope of our walk and give people a reason to become fundraisers for us."

Walkers register through the organization's website as virtual walkers. Like actual walkers, virtual walkers are directed to firstgiving.com, where they can create their own personalized fundraising page. PCANY pays Firstgiving an annual fee for providing this service.

Another outside vendor, Democracy in Action (Washington, D.C.), handles event registration, e-mail marketing, contact management and other Web-based functions for a monthly fee, based on the number of supporters in PCANY's database.

"We were already using both of these vendors for other events," says Matrazzo, "so there wasn't any additional cost associated with adding virtual walkers. We were just finding a new use for technology and services we already had at our disposal."

This is the organization's first year of offering walkers this option. Matrazzo says the response so far has been light, but she is hopeful. "As we continue to promote the concept through e-mail and other channels, I'm hoping it will pick up. As with most events, the challenge is getting people involved. I'm hoping that a combination of persistence and creativity will result in an increased response."

Source: Jennifer Matrazzo, Associate Executive Director, Prevent Child Abuse New York, Albany, NY. Phone (518) 445-1273. E-mail: jmatrazzo@preventchildabuseny.org

53 Establish a Long-term Relationship With New Businesses

What do you do when a new business opens in your area? Go beyond sending the token potted plant and be the first nonprofit to bring the owner on board as a supporter.

But rather than running the risk of offending the new businessperson with a premature ask, look for ways to distinguish your organization from the rest by taking steps to establish a positive long-term relationship with the business owner and staff.

Take the following steps to solidify a positive relationship with your community's new businesses:

1. Have employees of your nonprofit on hand for the business's grand opening. Wear name tags or logo clothing that identify the organization you represent.

2. Send a personal welcome letter to the business owner or manager with no strings attached.

3. Host a quarterly breakfast or lunch for community newcomers. Use the occasion to provide a tour of your facilities and offer guests a small memento.

4. If the business executive is new to your community, offer to schedule some time to take him/her around and make introductions to community leaders.

5. Invite the new owner or manager to accompany you as a guest to any civic organizations to which you belong (e.g., Rotary, Sertoma, Optimists Club).

54 Reward Referrals

Whenever you get a referral, send a note of appreciation within 24 hours. Here's an added touch: Include a lottery ticket with a note that says, "Thanks a million — That's what you deserve to win!"

55 Blog Boosts Fundraising

How can an online conversation help your fund development efforts?

Essentially, a blog is a website, and each time you post an update, search engines see that as fresh content and give it a favorable ranking. So if you have a blog for your organization, you are increasing your chances of being found by those who may one day make a gift.

Link your blog to your website and vice versa for even more exposure.

What might you include as blog content that relates to fund development? There's no end to the possibilities. Here are just a few ideas:

✓ Thank those who have funded a recent project and update them on its status. How is it impacting those you serve?

✓ Use your blog to profile those served by your organization. Make a compelling case for why support can and is making a noticeable difference.

✓ Promote upcoming events that the public may want to attend.

✓ Invite your blog readers to vote on ever-changing topics: the next funding project, what they like most about your organization's work and more.

✓ Make a call for volunteers for an event or project.

✓ Make announcements: the kickoff for your annual fund, achieving a milestone, receipt of a major gift, the appointment of new staff, etc.

56 Foundation Pins Fundraising Hopes on Jewelry Sales

It all started with one decorative jewelry pin, many years ago.

Created by Designs by Lucinda (Portland, ME), the pin was brought to the attention of the Wentworth-Douglass Hospital Foundation by its executive director who had sold the jewelry pieces to raise funds at her prior organization.

In the years since, sales of the pins have brought in nearly $20,000 for the foundation, says Mary Herring, foundation coordinator. The pins are sold at internal and external events, as well as displayed and sold at three different display cases throughout the hospital.

Here's how the program works: Organizations can contact Designs by Lucinda through the company's website (www.lucinda.com/fundraising) or by phone to order a minimum of 40 single-design pins, at $7.60 per pin. Officials with Designs by Lucinda recommend selling the pins for $16 each, for a 110 percent profit.

Placing an order by phone offers additional flexibility, letting you choose 60 pins in three styles with free shipping.

People who sport Lucinda pins become ambassadors for nonprofits through the conversations they start, according to the company's website.

Herring says she agrees with the pin's power to raise awareness, adding that the foundation places stickers on the card to which the pins are attached, allowing them to share more about their mission and activities.

Source: Mary Herring, Foundation Coordinator, Wentworth-Douglass Hospital Foundation, Dover, NH. Phone (603) 740-2581. E-mail: Mary.Herring@wdhospital.com

57 One Easy Way to Make Weddings Work for You

Today, planning a wedding often goes beyond choosing the venue, color schemes and flowers to choosing a worthy charity to celebrate on the big day as well.

What do you do when a couple calls to say they would like to use their wedding as a way to support your cause? Are you prepared to offer opportunities for their guests to do so?

If you don't have any formal programs set up to make weddings work for you, suggest that the bride and groom do an old-fashioned dollar dance, with the money going to benefit your organization instead of the bride and groom.

58 Side-by-side Illustration Moves Donors to Give

Joette Rosato, director, Seton Hall Fund, Seton Hall University (South Orange, NJ), wanted to create a visual to make people really think about what making a donation means:

"After working in alumni relations for seven years and moving on to development, I felt there was something missing in the way people think about donating. So I started thinking about the process of education of donors and thought that might be a good route to go."

That feeling, along with results of an alumni attitudinal survey, led Rosato to use an illustration of water glasses bearing logos of Seton Hall and five other Big East schools, each filled to reflect that college's giving rates (shown below). Seton Hall measured in at 8 percent, the lowest of all the schools.

Rosato and university officials used the visual in many mediums, including print, Web and e-mail. They incorporated the comparisons into the university's spring appeal, as ads on the university's website and used it for a smaller appeal involving the alumni board of directors.

Rosato says the giving statistics surprised many people, and that the illustration had the desired impact.

"Seton Hall alumni, students, parents and friends are a proud group of people, so the pride is there," Rosato says. The challenge in encouraging gifts "is getting them to take the next step. Many think that the other guy is donating, so why should they? This comparison showed them that, obviously, isn't the case."

Source: Joette Rosato, Director, Seton Hall Fund, Seton Hall University, South Orange, NJ. Phone (973) 378-2655. E-mail: Joette.Rosato@shu.edu

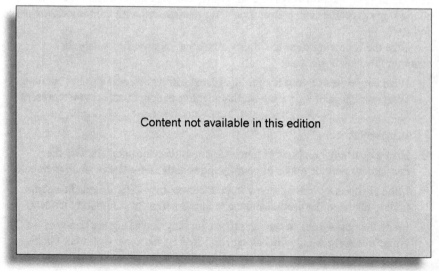

Content not available in this edition

59 Test Cold Calling as a Way to Acquire New Donors

Whether you'd like to bring in year-end dollars to boost your 2011 bottom line or start 2012 ahead of the game, one tried-and-true technique to consider is the cold call.

Calling current and former donors through annual phonathons is one reliable way nonprofits can renew gifts from these proven supporters. So why not test a targeted cold-call phoning effort exclusively aimed at nondonors?

Whether you use paid callers or volunteers, one caller or a dozen, conduct the effort over a two-week period or use a longer-term approach, be sure to create a script aimed at generating first-time gifts from those who have never given before. To achieve success:

1. **Select three funding projects from which donors can choose** rather than asking for general support. People like knowing how their gifts will be used, and your success rate will increase by offering clear-cut funding projects.

2. **Start small.** Ask for a modest gift — $15 or $25 — just to get these new individuals on board. Many people refuse to give just because they feel their modest contributions won't be appreciated or make any noticeable difference.

3. **Make it easy to give.** Offer credit card payments, installment payments — limit the number of payments for smaller gifts — and one-time cash payments.

4. **Offer special incentives.** Consider offering two or three inexpensive premiums for giving: free admission to an event, one-year membership in one of your clubs at a reduced rate or a calendar with photos that relate to your organization and its mission.

Your goal should be simply to acquire new donors regardless of gift size. Once that's accomplished you can focus on building a habit of giving.

Use this generic script aimed at nondonors as a starting point to create one for your cause:

Sample Phonathon Script Used for Nondonors

Caller:
Mr. Hansen, this is Marci Wiggins calling on behalf of the Acme Gospel Mission.

We're making a special effort this year to contact every citizen in our community to invite support for one of three special funding projects — and we're not asking for much.

Specifically, we would like you to consider a $15 or $25 gift to support one of these important projects:

1. New bedding for those who need shelter at our facility.
2. Meals for those we serve. A gift of $15 will cover meal costs for one needy person for one day.
3. Counseling services gifts to help get our visitors back on track.

Mr. Hansen, if you could find it in your heart to make a $15 or $25 gift for any one of these projects, you will receive two donated tickets for the Feb. 15 circus performance at Acme Auditorium. Which of these worthwhile projects would you like to fund today?

---

60 Expand Your Donor Base

To get more people making annual contributions, ask willing employees to submit names and addresses of family and friends. Then develop a direct mail appeal that invites in tribute gifts honoring any employee's tenure with your nonprofit. This concept can also be retooled to solicit gifts from friends of your volunteers.

61 Set Getting Expectations for Board Members

Having difficulty convincing board members to raise annual support on behalf of your cause? Set clear expectations.

In addition to their own giving, you may want individual board members to assume responsibility for getting annual gifts from friends and associates. To encourage that, share ways in which they can make that happen. Offer examples of how they could meet individual getting goals, such as:

- Establishing a challenge gift for friends and associates, "I'll match whatever you give up to $X."

- Selling a minimum of X tickets to a fundraising event.

- Hosting a $X per person dinner at your home.

- Convincing a minimum of X businesses to write a check or provide a gift in kind of products or services.

Sometimes board members are willing to ask others for support; they simply want some options for how they can make that happen.

62 Bolster Year-end Gifts

For any nonprofit that acquires books, offering donors the opportunity to have a book plate with a designated honoree's name on it will help garner additional gifts and engage donors.

63 Form Ambassador Clusters In Neighboring Communities

If your nonprofit serves communities outside of your city, form ambassador groups in those areas to assist with fund development. To get such groups up and running:

1. Ask persons in surrounding communities who already support your cause to join that community's ambassador advisory group. To encourage their involvement, explain that the group's purpose goes far beyond fund development. In addition to assisting with prospect identification, cultivation, solicitation and stewardship of current donors, they will be expected to make the public more aware of the positive ways in which your organization serves the community.
2. Have each community's group meet quarterly to learn more about your organization and to plan and support activities for that community: Host an educational program, plan a special event or after-hours reception, identify and review names of prospective donors, plan stewardship calls to thank other current donors and more.

Over time, the attention you give to forming and supporting the efforts of ambassador groups in those communities you serve will result in broadening the level of support for your organization.

64 Move Sponsors to Increasing Levels of Support

To increase the number of sponsors for various aspects of your organization (e.g., events and programs) and to increase existing sponsors' levels of yearly support, create a ladder of sponsorship opportunities to which you can refer.

List all available sponsorship opportunities in least- to most-expensive order. Each increasing level of sponsorship should include more attractive benefits.

When calling on new prospects, offer less-costly sponsorship opportunities to get them on board with your organization. Invite those with a history of sponsorships to move to a higher level sponsorship opportunity that will include more exclusive benefits.

65 'Simple but Powerful' Video Proves to be Invaluable Fundraising Tool

A video presentation is credited with helping The Holland Hospital Foundation (Holland, MI) add 20 new businesses to its donor ranks and increase its donor base by 40 percent during a time of recession.

Foundation Executive Director Sue Ann Culp says, "Michigan has the second largest unemployment rate in the nation, and still, we have experienced increases, unlike other nonprofits in this area who are struggling to survive."

Culp credits that growth, in part, to a "simple but powerful" video presentation.

Created using Microsoft PowerPoint, the video includes the foundation's mission statement and an overview of its three focus areas of funding: 1) school nursing, 2) the community health center, and 3) the community nurse who serves at a local homeless shelter for women and children. The video includes statistics supporting community need, usage and outcome for each area, as well as dollars needed to sustain the services. It concludes with a plea for help and contact information.

All staff carry the presentation on flash drives, on their laptops and in DVD and DVR formats to share with prospects. Culp says they also send the DVD to donors.

Foundation officials show the video in presentations to corporations, businesses, grantors and prospective donors, as well as at community gatherings like chamber of commerce breakfasts. They highlight it at the foundation's major community fundraising events and in orientations for hospital employees and physicians.

The communications tool is proving invaluable for the foundation, Culp says, especially given its low production cost. "The only cost associated with producing this presentation was staff time, and a disc of stock photos. Its shelf life is infinite as long as our focus areas remain the same, since we can easily change statistics and numbers year to year."

For organizations seeking to invest time and effort in a similar video project, Culp recommends adding elements exclusive to your organization.

"We have named our mission The FACE of Holland Project, Funding Access to Care for Everyone, so the images we used in our video are lots of faces, and faces draw the viewer in. The background song is 'The Prayer' by Celtic Woman, which reflects the deep religious overtones of this community without being overtly denominational.

"The trick to producing a presentation of this type is to make sure the message, music and imaging are strongly emotional, personal and cohesive, so it flows seamlessly," she says. "The ask at the end is the natural culmination of the presentation, and the evidence of need is overwhelming. The pictures tell the story better than any narrator could."

Source: Sue Ann Culp, Executive Director, Holland Hospital Foundation, Holland, MI. Phone (616) 355-3974. E-mail: saculp@hollandhospital.org

66 Keep Floating New Funding Ideas

Rather than constantly marketing the same old thing, keep testing new funding ideas among potential donors. Change funding choices on a monthly basis or float particular ideas to targeted prospects or offer a menu of three different gift options from which donors can choose.

By continually testing new funding opportunities, along with varying gift ranges, you can uncover gift alternatives that may be far more popular than others. And if a particular gift suggestion takes hold, keep offering it as a gift option.

67 Specific Telefund Ask Boosts New Donor Gifts

Organizers of the Telefund phonathon efforts for Boston University (Boston, MA) increased new donors by 100 percent by asking new donors to make a gift equal to their graduation year in dollars and cents.

"We doubled our number of new donors from the previous year because of how we approached their ask amounts," says Alison Werner, Telefund program manager. "The amount — $19.90 for a 1990 graduate, for example — was accessible and cutesy enough to get their attention. Most donors figured it was the cost of a dinner out."

Werner says they haven't seen as much growth in the number of new donors this year, but attributes that to the fact that they had so much growth the previous year.

Source: Alison Werner, Program Manager, Telefund, Boston University, Boston, MA. Phone (617) 358-1199. E-mail: awerner@bu.edu

68 Every Student Helps Raise Funds at Calvin College

At Calvin College (Grand Rapids, MI), the annual fund is really about every student, says Director of Annual Giving Souzan Karadsheh. To convey that message, college officials created the Every Student Challenge.

"We wanted donors to know that their gifts impact the experience of every student, every day," Karadsheh says. "The challenge was a vehicle to communicate to our alumni and friends about the Calvin Annual Fund and the importance of supporting every student."

To underscore this message, college officials tied their challenge goal to the number of enrolled students, seeking to reach 4,092 new or upgraded donors. They created campaign graphics featuring faces of Calvin students, along with students' own words about the heart of their Calvin experience.

These images carried the simple message through Calvin's publications, its website, ads in the alumni magazine, articles online and video and electronic messaging.

Karadsheh says the challenge proved highly successful, as they exceeded their goal by nearly 3,000 gifts. An important part of that success, the director of annual giving notes, was studying their program and highlighting areas of need, which led to a positive response of support for the students: "We received various notes and other communication from alumni and friends sharing their enthusiasm for the challenge and articulating their interest in supporting students. I think it was important for the students to learn that such an initiative existed to support them."

Source: Souzan Karadsheh, Director of Annual Giving, Calvin College, Grand Rapids, MI. Phone (616) 526-8442. E-mail: sk2@calvin.edu

69 Engage Awards Recipients

Once you've made awards to individuals or organizations, don't stop there. Work to build a long-term relationship. Get the award recipients involved in your cause by asking them to help identify future recipients.

70 To Better Target Prospects, Segment List

People contribute based on their interests. To appeal to their interests, it's important that you segment your list.

Whether you are creating direct mail appeals or coordinating a phonathon effort, targeting segmented groups will increase your gift response rate.

Make time to analyze your existing constituency list and prioritize segmentation opportunities that can be tested throughout the year.

Here are a few segmentation examples:

- Married with no children.
- Occupation.
- Place of residence (ZIP code).
- Gender, race, religion.
- Avocation.
- Age.
- Political interests.
- Family-owned businesses.
- Widows/widowers.
- Art collection owners.
- Land rich individuals.
- Persons with a second residence.

Explore the possibilities, then match various groups with giving opportunities.

71 Why Do People Give?

What motivates people to give? Do you attempt to pin that down each time you successfully close a gift? Some of the key gift motivators for giving include:

✓ Acceptance
✓ Altruism
✓ Appreciation
✓ Being asked
✓ Gratitude
✓ Group support
✓ Return on investment
✓ Sympathy
✓ Happiness
✓ Pain, grief, guilt

72 Fundraising Brochures Should Be Written to Sell

How does the content of your fundraising brochures stand up against the competition? Same old, same old? A great brochure should be a powerful sales tool. Win over more contributors by focusing on:

- **Persuasion rather than information.** Rather than featuring facts about your organization and its "products," focus on an intriguing idea that positions your cause and makes a compelling case for support.

- **The donor rather than your needs.** What's in it for the person making the gift? How will making a gift benefit him/her?

- **Action.** Incorporate messages that direct the reader to take specific action: "Help improve your community's quality of life by making your gift today!"

73 Partner With Another Nonprofit For Mutually Profitable Event

Looking for a way to generate $10,000 or more in new funds? Partner with another nonprofit with a mission different from your own to organize a joint fundraising event that will benefit both organizations equally, both in added funds and added exposure.

People love to see collaboration among nonprofit organizations, even when it's a fundraising event. Co-hosting a special event with another nonprofit will provide mutual benefits, including:

1. Exposing your nonprofit to attendees who might not otherwise be familiar with or support your efforts.

2. Having at least twice as much volunteer involvement in planning and coordinating the event — maybe more if additional nonprofits are involved — making the event a bit less labor-intensive.

3. Generating additional needed funds to help meet your annual fundraising goal or support a special project or immediate need.

74 Calendar Project Raises Eyebrows While Raising Funds

What do you call an auto dealer standing naked except for a strategically placed hubcap? Or a real estate agent enjoying a cigar and glass of wine with nothing more than a For Sale sign for cover?

The Greater Westerly-Pawcatuck Chamber of Commerce (Westerly, RI) calls it fundraising.

"They're all chamber members and basically naked except for a prop representing their business to cover their 'business,'" says Lisa Konicki, chamber executive director, of the chamber's popular Men of Westerly calendar fundraiser. "They get some great publicity, they help the chamber, and they raise money for some good causes, too."

The fundraiser, now in its second year, is planned and produced by the chamber, but proceeds are shared with several local charities, adding to its appeal and area impact.

The 2010 calendar features 33 local businessmen of all shapes and sizes ranging in age from late 20s to early 70s.

"It's not about physical appearance," says Konicki, recalling the standing ovation received by the calendar's two over-70 models. "Featuring people with a solid reputation in the community, guys everybody knows and loves, is what really makes it work."

Because models are sworn to secrecy and photographed outside normal business hours, speculation fuels much of the buzz surrounding the event. A gala event — Men of Westerly Revealed — taps this curiosity with a grand reveal of the participating businessmen and an unveiling of the new calendar.

"Done right, it's something the community can really get behind," Konicki says, noting that 2009 calendar sales, combined with ticket sales, sponsorship and advertising, netted around $13,000. "It's fun, humorous and all about having a big heart."

Source: Lisa Konicki, Executive Director, The Greater Westerly-Pawcatuck Chamber of Commerce, Westerly, RI. Phone (800) 732-7636. E-mail: Lkonicki@westerlychamber.org. Website: www.westerlychamber.org

75   Text Donations Offer New Way to Talk About, Generate Gifts

In March 2010, staff at the Brooklyn Public Library (Brooklyn, NY) began accepting donations via text message. The undertaking was part of their Support Our Shelves campaign, an annual drive to raise money for library materials.

Jason Carey, director of marketing, says they thought text donations might attract potential donors for whom getting to the library is not always convenient. "We already had a separate texting technology to notify when materials were overdue, or when guests could pick up books," he says. "To introduce a donation element seemed like a natural progression."

- **How text donations work:** The Brooklyn Public Library chose to use mGive (a product of Mobile Accord, Denver, CO) — the same company that hosted text donations to victims of the Haitian earthquake. Donors use their phones to send a text to a predetermined number and specify how much they would like to donate. The system includes a widget for the library's website — donors click the widget and donate by entering a code. Additionally, mGive offers a Facebook widget, and other social networking tools to get the text donation program in public view.

- **Cost:** The library had to apply to be included in the service (see mGive's charitable participation standards, in the box, below) and pay a one-time setup fee of $500. Library staff then chose among three monthly packages ($399 bronze, $649 silver and $1,499 gold), and paid corresponding transaction fees (35 cents plus 3.5 percent bronze, 32 cents plus 3.5 percent silver or 30 cents plus 3.5 percent gold).

- **The Result:** Carey says the new program has so far produced modest results, but its implications are far-reaching. "The key thing we've seen so far is it's a great way to get a new contingent of supporters involved with the library," he says. "It's a new way to talk about fundraising." By signing up for the program, potential donors are automatically put in contact with Carey and his marketing services; even the simple novelty of text-donation technology has attracted a new audience to cultivate as donors. Carey says he aims to add a sense of urgency to marketing for text donations. "When we give donors a reason to feel they need to give immediately, that will be the best way to utilize this as a tool."

Source: Jason Carey, Director of Marketing, Brooklyn Public Library, Brooklyn, NY. Phone (718)230-2209. E-mail: j.carey@brooklynpubliclibrary.org. Website: brooklynpubliclibrary.org

Content not available in this edition

76   Referral Tip

At the onset of board meetings, pass out index cards. Ask board members to write down their names along with three prospects they believe worthy of cultivation. Have them place an asterisk (*) next to the names of prospects they would be willing to approach with you.

77   Online Giving Tip

To encourage immediate contributions, have a GIVE NOW button on your website's home page and as many other pages as you can justify. The GIVE NOW button should take visitors directly to a donation landing page to minimize clicks.

78   Boost Your Annual Fund

Try this annual fund strategy to increase giving among greater numbers of donors:

In your fiscal year's third quarter, send an appreciation letter to current donors, updating them on your annual fund totals and thanking them for their valuable support. Then invite them to share an enclosed over-the-top list of budget needs (and return envelope) with a friend or associate, explaining that, if your nonprofit is fortunate enough to meet its annual fund goal, additional gifts received by year end will address those special funding needs you have identified.

79 Create a Call Strategy

Getting into a routine will help ensure you regularly make prospect calls. One way to better manage prospect-calling procedures, begin your appointment-setting measures three weeks before the call.

Three weeks out, prioritize who merits a call. Two weeks out, set appointments. The final week, make calls.

80 $10,000 Sponsorship Ideas

Here are four sponsorship ideas any organization could use to generate an additional $10,000 or more:

1. **Sponsor an existing project/program.** Take an inventory of programs that presently exist. Could any of them be sponsored?

2. **Sponsor your communications effort.** For example, use the sponsorship gifts to underwrite the cost of your regularly published newsletter or magazine. Include the names of the sponsors on the inside cover of each issue saying, "This publication is brought to you by..."

3. **Sponsor something new.** Get your sponsors to underwrite a new revenue-generating project, so their gifts can create new gifts. Examples include: a special event, hiring a new part-time position, etc.

4. **Identify 11 businesses each capable of contributing $1,000.** Approach each and invite them to serve as sponsors of a program or event you have identified as worthy of their support. Ten of the $1,000 gifts will be used to generate $10,000 in needed revenue, while the 11th will be used to underwrite benefits for each of the 11 sponsors.

81 Make Time to Forge New Relationships

New fiscal year getting underway? Make time to establish new donor relationships now rather than scrambling to solicit first-time gifts late in the year. Begin with a plan that includes the following elements:

1. **Identify who you want to approach.** What's a realistic number of new prospects to cultivate? What's your criteria for who makes it onto your list?

2. **Establish a timeline that includes introduction/cultivation strategies for each identified prospect.** Include the name of the staff person, board member or volunteer responsible for managing the cultivation of each individual.

3. **Put your plan into action.** Who will call on whom? How will you work to involve each prospect in the life of your organization?

4. **Make the ask.** Depending on each prospect's readiness to invest, invite each to make a gift as you move further into your year. Offer multiple funding options.

82 Present a Powerful Pitch With First-person Details

When Dr. Talia Witkowski speaks to potential donors on behalf of Heal Your Hunger (Los Angeles, CA), a nonprofit dedicated to helping people with eating disorders and addictions, people pay attention. Not only is Witkowski volunteer outreach coordinator for the group; two-and-a-half years ago she was one of their clients, using their valuable services, she says, to turn her life around completely.

Witkowski shares tips for bringing your organization's mission to life by sharing powerful, personal anecdotes:

❑ **Tell them why only this group was able to help you.** Witkowski tells people that she did seek out more traditional means of help before finding what she needed at Heal Your Hunger. "I want to show them that there are some limits to that world," she says, "and that Heal Your Hunger was what finally worked."

❑ **Talk about the before, but always include the after.** Witkowski's story follows a narrative arc that anybody can appreciate: triumphing over the tragedies she once endured. It's not just about what happened to you; "I always talk about what happened for me because I received treatment," Witkowski says.

❑ **Talk only until they start talking.** During Witkowski's presentations, it's a guarantee that her audience "will start telling me how they want to help, or maybe tell me about someone they know who's hurting," she says. No matter how refined and rehearsed your speech, cut it short once others are so engaged that they want to take over the conversation. There's no better way to let someone feel a personal attachment to your organization.

❑ **Keep it short, stupid!** Even though Heal Your Hunger's work is something she could talk about for hours, "I talk for maybe five, 10 minutes in total," Witkowski says. If an individual wants to hear more, he or she will likely seek you out on a one-to-one basis, which is the perfect opportunity to ask for a significant contribution.

Source: Dr. Talia Witkowski, Volunteer Outreach Coordinator, Heal Your Hunger, Los Angeles, CA. Phone (310) 281-8831. E-mail: dr.taliawitkowski@yahoo.com

83 Planning Boosts Class Agent Program

While a class agent program can require a large investment of time, it can pay off in terms of keeping people connected to your cause.

"A class agent program can be a great way to keep alumni connected with their classmates and increase networking possibilities," says Sue Drilling, director of special programs at Luther College (Decorah, IA). She oversees the college's 100-member class agent program. "The personal touch class agents provide through their letters lends greater meaning and purpose to the college's fundraising appeal, creating stronger bonds to the college, which can translate into better alumni events and a desire to contribute gifts, so current students have a great Luther College experience, too."

The key to a smoothly run program, says Drilling, is planning. Luther officials created a class agent handbook they give to volunteer class agents at their annual luncheon during homecoming week. The 27-page handbook helps prepare class agents, addresses questions and acts as a reference for agents. It includes information about the college's three-hour class agent luncheon, program and preparation workshop; policies and procedures; sample class agent and class reunion letters; and a dates-to-remember class agent calendar, along with references, giving statistics and reports.

Drilling says the handbook is proving to be a useful component of their class agent program. "It's much easier to respond to the many questions from agents and provide the support they'll need to do their jobs, when it's all laid out in advance."

Source: Sue Drilling, Director of Special Programs, Luther College, Decorah, IA. Phone (563) 387-1100. E-mail: drillisu@luther.edu

This excerpt from the class agent handbook for Luther College (Decorah, IA) shows a sample class reunion letter, one of the tools included in the handbook to aid class agents in connecting with alumni:

Content not available in this edition

Tips for Class Agent Program Success

Ben Campbell, associate director of annual giving, Lawrence University (Appleton, WI) manages 100 volunteers through the class agent program, some of whom have been class agents for 50 years. Here, Campbell shares six tips to make a class agent program successful:

1. **Volunteers should be loyal to and passionate about your cause.** If persons are going to ask you to consider a gift, she says, you hope they will practice what they preach. "It's important they share why they give and how that will help us reach out to other folks."

2. **Volunteers are a valuable resource.** Ask existing agents whom to recruit as class agents. They know what the job requires and who would be a good fit. Ask also how you can make it easier for them to do their jobs and how you can make the program better.

3. **Communications should be positive and personal —not all about the money.** By sharing information about their lives since they left school or sharing favorite memories, class agents build a bridge between themselves, prospective donors and the university.

4. **Volunteers should be treated similarly, but differently.** Knowing agents' preferences can help them do their job better, Campbell says. For example, some like daily reminders as it's getting close to a deadline, while others want to be contacted exclusively by e-mail.

5. **Volunteers should be informed.** Share updated statistics to help class agents do their job (e.g., where their class is donation-wise, etc.) and university news so they know how the money they are helping to raise is being used.

6. **Giving histories matter.** Your most loyal and consistent supporters, especially at your leadership giving levels, are likely to make some of your best agents. They obviously feel strongly about giving and will be able to legitimately convey the importance of it to prospective donors.

Source: Benjamin C. Campbell, Associate Director of Annual Giving, Lawrence University, Appleton, WI. Phone (920) 832-6936. E-mail: benjamin.c.campbell@lawrence.edu

84 Expand Your Donor Base by 20 Percent

What would it take to expand the number of current contributors by 20 percent? First, multiply the number of last fiscal year's contributors by 20 percent (1,000 donors times 20 percent equals 200.) Once you know that number, prepare an action plan that identifies what your staff will need to do to generate your 20 percent.

Examples of action plan strategies might include:

✓ Send three additional appeal letters to prospects who are not currently in the database.
✓ Conduct a week-long phonathon directed to nondonors (or outsource the job to a telemarketing firm).
✓ Host a series of get-to-know-us receptions inviting individuals who have never made a contribution.
✓ Coordinate a new special event aimed at attracting those with no prior history of giving.

85 Gift Memberships Engage Current Members

Offering gift memberships can be an effective way to grow your member-based organization. Here are examples of how two organizations are finding success doing so:

American Homebrewers Association (Boulder, CO):

Persons who want to give a one-year gift membership ($38) to the American Homebrewers Association (AHA) purchase an AHA gift card on the association's website. The gift cards have increased gift memberships by 300 percent, says Director Gary Glass.

The gift card is affixed to a mailable paper holder that contains "To" and "From" fields and an area for personalization. The gift card/holder is mailed to the gift giver, who then mails it to the gift membership recipient. The recipient visits a website and uses a code printed on the gift card to validate the membership. Once a gift membership is validated, the person receiving it is mailed a new member packet.

Glass says they originally used the gift cards in home brew supply stores to attract new members, but their ease of use prompted AHA officials to start using the cards for gift memberships about two years ago.

"Rather than having the member give us the gift member's contact information and mailing address, the person who receives the gift card fills out their information, which reduces the chance for errors," Glass says. "It also allows us to shorten the turnaround time to process a gift membership from three weeks to three days. All we have to do is mail out a gift card/card holder to the gift giver and they do the rest."

Adventure Cycling Association (Missoula, MT):

The annual Share the Cycling Joy membership recruitment campaign for the Adventure Cycling Association (Missoula, MT) has increased gift memberships by 25 percent in two years, says Julie Huck, membership director. The year-round effort offers members the opportunity to win prizes — including a shopping spree at the association's online gift shop — for giving gift memberships and/or encouraging cyclists to join.

"We pulled together existing elements like our send-a-friend sample issue and holiday gift programs and developed the Share the Cycling Joy program around them," Huck says. "Because of the time it takes to develop the infrastructure for this type of system, an important part of creating it was the ability to use it for multiple years."

Members participate by giving a gift membership ($40 except October - December, when cost is $20; see story, left) or by using an online form to send a sample issue of the association's magazine or e-mail that allows a friend to request a free issue.

The association promotes the gift membership campaign with a member magazine ad, article in its bi-weekly e-newsletter to 40,000 member and non-member subscribers, on its website (www.adventurecycling.org/joy), in blog posts, on the association's Facebook page, in an October e-mail and in a printed piece in November.

Sources: Gary Glass, Director, American Homebrewers Association, Boulder, CO. Phone (888) 822-6273, ext. 121. E-mail: gary@brewersassociation.org
Julie Huck, Membership & Development Director, Adventure Cycling Association, Missoula, MT. Phone (800) 755-2453 ext. 214. E-mail: jhuck@adventurecycling.org

Limited-time Appeal Encourages Gift Memberships

Persons who wish to give a gift membership to the Adventure Cycling Association (Missoula, MT) can do so year-round for $40 (see story, right). But each October through December, they can make the same gift at half the price — just in time for holiday gift giving, says Julie Huck, membership director.

"We promote our holiday gift membership program through e-mail, with messages in our e-newsletter and with a mailing piece sent to members in November," Huck says. The mailing piece includes a letter introducing the program, a form to renew their membership and give gifts, and a return envelope.

Gift membership recipients receive a card with a personal message from the donor and membership card prior to receiving their new member packet, which is mailed about a week later.

In January, new gift members who joined during the holiday campaign receive a special welcome e-mail.

In 2009, new and renewing members gave 462 gift memberships (275 at half price and 187 at full price) during the association's holiday gift membership program, says Huck, noting that the retention rate among gift members is about 28 percent.

86 Boost Your Donor Participation Rate

Colleges and universities often strive to increase the percentage of alumni who support their institutions on an annual basis. Other types of nonprofits should do the same using their database (mailing list) as the starting point.

Let's assume you want to increase donor participation by 7 percent over the prior year's participation rate of 28 percent. To be sure you are on target with your goal midway through the year, multiply your total database number by the desired participation rate, in this case 35 percent, to determine the number of donors needed.

Assuming your total prospect pool amounts to 10,000 names, for example, you would need 3,500 donors by year end to meet your goal.

Breaking goals down can help determine appropriate strategies needed to reach them.

87 Online Search Tool Promotes Matching Gift Opportunities

Sometimes, the potential to double a donor gift is just a mouse click away.

Visitors to the website for KUHF Houston Public Radio (Houston, TX) can use an online search tool to quickly learn if their company has a matching gift program.

Using the Employer Matching Gift search tool offered by HEP Development (Leesburg, VA), visitors to www.kuhf.org enter their company name into the search bar. Search results include:

- ❑ Company.
- ❑ Subsidiary of.
- ❑ Foundation #.
- ❑ When information was last updated.
- ❑ Matching gift program contact person.
- ❑ Phone and e-mail address for the matching gift program.
- ❑ Matching Gift Form URL.
- ❑ Minimum amount matched.
- ❑ Maximum amount matched.
- ❑ Total amount matched per employee.
- ❑ Gift ratio.
- ❑ A comments section.
- ❑ Matching gifts procedure.

HEP staff maintain and regularly update the list of matching gift companies.

Suzanne Tullis, KUHF director of individual giving, says they have used the search tool for two years. "We used to have to keep the list of companies that provide matching gifts up-to-date ourselves and then regularly mail it to our constituents," she says. "This is a more convenient, simple and cost-saving solution."

Stephen P. Hafner, HEP Development founder and CEO, says the search tool is just one important part of an overall best-practices matching gift strategy. Other services include appending employer data for nonprofits and then determining if the firm is match-eligible which allows the nonprofit to grow its pool of match revenue.

"We can also mine a nonprofit's existing employer data to see if the company matches, so that they can target the donor for a match," he says. The search tool is also a stand-alone product, says Hafner, selling for $600 to $1,000 per year.

Sources: Stephen P. Hafner, Founder & CEO, HEP Development, Leesburg, VA. Phone (800) 681-4438. E-mail: steve@hepdata.com. Website: www.hepdata.com Suzanne Tullis, Director of Individual Giving, KUHF Houston Public Radio, Houston, TX. Phone (713) 743-7491. E-mail: stullis@kuhf.org

88 Gift Club Idea

To help build a habit of giving among first-time donors, consider establishing a gift club that requires three or more consecutive years of giving: "Membership in The Emerald Club is open to anyone who makes an annual contribution for three or more consecutive years."

89 Seeking First-time Gifts? Consider Monthly Appeal

Looking to expand your annual contributor list? Consider a personalized appeal sent to different groups of nondonors each month of the year. Directing a highly personalized letter to a different group of nondonors each month, you can:

- ✓ Target specific groups of individuals and/or businesses each month (e.g., particular ZIP codes, professions, interest groups).
- ✓ Make your letter more timely. If you're preparing a November letter, for example, your message might make reference to Thanksgiving.
- ✓ Test different appeal letters and funding projects to determine which produce the best responses.
- ✓ Generate new gift revenue on an ongoing basis. Instead of two different appeals going out twice each year, this approach, if successful, should provide your organization with ongoing gift revenue from new sources.

90 Share Your List Of Memorial Gift Opportunities

If you want people to consider your organization for memorial gifts, develop a wide-ranging wish list of memorial gift opportunities to draw from when those times arise.

Turn to your memorial gifts committee to help identify gift opportunities. Develop a simple memorial gift opportunities brochure to share with families and distribute to appropriate locations: churches, synagogues and funeral homes. You may also wish to include the brochure (or the list) in other mailings to make your constituency aware of those memorial opportunities.

What might your memorial gifts brochure include? Consider these possibilities:

- A brief description of your organization's mission and services.

- A list of memorial gift opportunities that includes brief descriptions and costs.

- A list of memorials received during the past fiscal year.

- A statement of how memorials will be recognized.

- A panel that the recipient can fill out, detach and return with a memorial gift.

- Contact information for anyone wishing to explore a memorial gift.

Be sure to include a wide range of gift amounts and opportunities, and review the list as often as quarterly to remove items that have been selected and address new needs.

91 Committee of 100 Generates $50,000

Want to generate more $500 gifts for your annual fund? Here's an idea:

1. Initiate an exclusive annual gift club for anyone willing to make an annual contribution of $500 and give it a name such as The Committee of 100.

2. Anyone who gives at that level gets the privilege of voting how they wish to have their donations used based on recommendations from staff. Committee members choose how they wish their donations to be spent.

3. To increase membership in your Committee of 100, send an appeal directed to a targeted group of would-be donors and/or coordinate a phonathon. In addition, host special receptions for key individuals in your community or targeted areas that include a brief program outlining the committee's goals.

If successful, your Committee of 100 will result in $50,000 in gifts directed to a funding project (or projects) that the group has collectively chosen.

92 Give Structure to Volunteer-driven Fundraising

If your shop is striving to build greater volunteer involvement in various aspects of fund development, it's wise to create an organizational structure that helps visualize who does what and who reports to whom. Such organizational charts will vary from nonprofit to nonprofit depending on types of volunteer committees and fund development priorities.

An organizational chart such as this will help staff to better manage volunteer programs and will also be useful in expanding volunteer involvement.

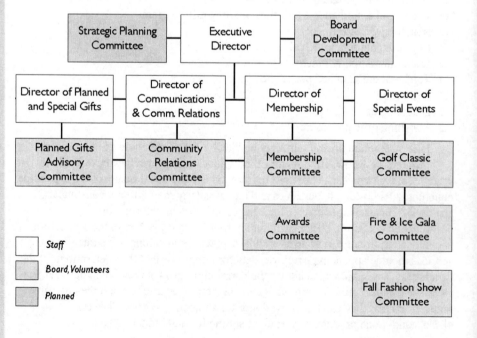

93 Five Ways to Acquire More First-time Donors

Looking for ways to garner more annual contributors? Test any or all of these ideas to determine what works best for you:

1. **Direct mail appeals.** Do some testing to targeted groups (e.g., businesses, ZIP codes) to measure response rates, then go with what's working best.

2. **Greater volunteer involvement.** Try involving volunteers in various capacities to find out what works best: city-wide annual fund campaign, board development committee, special events committee, etc.

3. **Telesolicitation.** Try outsourcing some of your mailing list to a telemarketing firm and compare results with having a pool of volunteers or your own paid callers do the job. Test targeted groups and different funding projects to see which produces the best results.

4. **Online giving.** Conduct some e-campaigns to targeted groups. Offer funding invitations on your website that include changing wish lists of needs and special giving incentives.

5. **Face-to-face calls.** Set a goal to make a minimum number of calls to new prospects each week or each month.

94 10 Ways to Get Out and Make Those Calls

Do you get caught up in administrative bureaucracy that prevents you from making important cultivation and solicitation calls?

Whether others are keeping you tied to the office or procrastination is holding you back, here are some tips to help you break away and focus on what matters most: raising needed money.

1. Designate one or more days of each week to be scheduled out of the office and making calls.

2. Set Friday afternoons aside to do nothing but schedule a minimum number of appointments, regardless of when they are to take place.

3. Delegate in-house (administrative) duties to the highest degree possible.

4. Be open to early morning and after-work appointments that still allow you to attend to office demands.

5. Inform your supervisor of scheduled appointments in advance to prevent internal meeting conflicts.

6. If your work requires long-distance trips, map out geographic regions you intend to visit throughout the year.

7. Create a yearlong cultivation/solicitation schedule for all major gift prospects.

8. Come up with a staff competition — that includes your CEO — for the most completed visits each week, month and year.

9. Meet weekly with staff and/or develop a reporting form to review attempted appointments, confirmed appointments and completed calls.

10. To increase employee awareness of the importance of contacting prospects, have every employee accompany you — or another member of the development staff — on one call each year.

Maintain good records of completed appointments each year as a way to measure performance.

95 Boost Workplace Giving

Get creative to encourage staff giving.

For example, give every employee who pledges a minimum gift to your workplace campaign a chance to pop a balloon filled with a slip of paper identifying one of several donated prizes (e.g., a free day off, event tickets, restaurant gift certificates, movie passes, preferred parking space for a month).

96 Partner With an Image-hungry Business

Consider forming a mutually beneficial alliance with businesses in your community that could stand to improve their images or gain a reputation for philanthropy.

Meet with officials of these businesses to explore project possibilities that enhance their public image and raise funds for your nonprofit. Your proposal of possibilities might include:

- A special fundraising event sponsored and staffed by the business.

- Use of their facilities and/or services by your organization.

- A public pledge that the business intends to donate a specific amount of employee time toward volunteer efforts with your organization.

- A commitment to underwrite start-up costs of a new program.

Be sure that your proposal includes tangible benefits geared toward the business being approached: number of news releases, television and radio opportunities, sponsorship signage, incentives for employee participation and more.

97 Increase Online Giving

To increase online giving, develop ways to involve visitors with your website. Make your website involvement rich by adding features such as:

- Members-only interactive groups
- Online surveys
- Online threaded discussion groups
- Online chat groups or bulletin boards
- Chat sessions with experts
- Online book clubs
- Other affinity groups

98 Test Various Wish List Types

Wish lists can be a great way to get the word out to your supporters about your current and ongoing needs.

But what should you wish for?

Because wish lists generally represent needs that are not part of your current budget, you can afford to test different types of funding opportunities over time to decide which works best for you.

Here are some examples of wish list variations to consider either separately or in some combination:

- Capital projects
- Equipment needs
- Supplies
- Named endowment opportunities
- Gifts for new "seed" programs
- Client-centered gifts (for those you serve) such as scholarships, financial aid or internships
- Employee grants for professional development

99 Create Collaborative Competition With Your Rival

Does your nonprofit have a rival organization? If so, why not collaborate to create a friendly competition among both organizations' supporters? That rivalry may help to motivate giving among both constituencies.

Here are some examples of how that might work:

✓ The organization showing the highest percentage giving over last year's total wins.

✓ The organization that generates the most in new $500-and-above gifts wins.

✓ The nonprofit that has the highest constituent participation rate in annual giving by year-end wins.

100 Involve Younger Constituents At a Summer Beach Party

Summer is vacation time for many potential donors, making it the perfect time for your organization to host a summer-fun fundraiser that celebrates your organization while attracting new donors.

Brian Kish, assistant vice president for advancement at Salve Regina University (Newport, RI) and annual giving consultant with Campbell & Company (Chicago, IL), says that one of the most important ways to promote annual giving is to attract younger donors.

"The earlier you can start engaging potential donors, the better," Kish says. The likelihood of a donor returning to donate to the same institution increases approximately 20 percent with each year of his/her engagement.

One proven way to attract younger people — both current and future donors — is to plan a fundraiser around an event they would want to attend anyway, Kish says. "You want people to be asking one another, 'Are you going to this event? Well then so am I.'"

Salve Regina hosts The Bash at the Beach — a seaside party in a historical and touristy part of town, he says. "We knew younger alumni would be around town during the summer, but wouldn't be coming to campus. So we decided to take the fundraising party to them."

For a summer bash, Kish recommends:

✓ Holding the event at a well-loved restaurant or bar with outdoor seating, a large deck or a waterfront view.

✓ Charging a ticket price that serves as the donor's contribution to the fundraiser. The ticket will earn the donor two drinks, food, parking and a gift. Build the fair market value of those items into the ticket price, with enough left over to earn a healthy percentage for your organization.

✓ Aiming your marketing techniques at younger donors — advertise in recent alumni publications, organizations for young professionals and online.

Source: Brian Kish, Assistant Vice President for Advancement, Salve Regina University, Newport, RI, and Annual Giving Consultant, Campbell & Company, Chicago, IL. Phone (401) 847-6650.
E-mail: annualGiving@campbellcompany.com and brian.kish@salve.edu.
Websites: www.salve.edu and www.campbellcompany.com/people/b_kish.html

101 — Offer Businesses Varied Gift Options

Wanting to broaden support from community and area businesses? Try offering different funding projects with the knowledge that some may be more appealing than others.

Whether you do it on a monthly or quarterly basis, develop a one- or two-page newsletter that includes varied funding projects each time it's sent out (or delivered) to businesses. In addition to the wish list of funding opportunities, your newsletter can include brief news items about your programs and services that may be of interest to businesses. Be sure to enclose a business reply envelope with each issue.

Sample page of a two-page newsletter distributed to businesses.

News for Area Businesses from ABC Nonprofit

Many thanks to the following businesses who contributed to last quarter's Support a Child effort:

- Acme Printing
- Beleme Brothers
- Dance Away
- Ely Manufacturing
- Tools & Tools
- Wheterhoos Services

ABC Nonprofit helped serve 544 underprivileged youth during the last quarter. Our efforts are helping enrich the lives of area youth who will one day be contributing members of this community and region.

Thanks to these businesses that donated in-kind services last quarter:

Bell's Printing   El Fredo Pizza
Heartland, Inc.   Tri-state Steel

2nd Quarter Funding Opportunities

We invite area businesses to help sponsor all or part of the Fall Field Trip for Youth. Some of the sponsorship opportunities associated with this annual field trip include:

Overall sponsor $10,000
Transportation $2,500
Attraction and educational fees $2,000
Food $200/child
Lodging $100/child
Supervision $50/child

See Page 2 for Sponsorship Benefits! Return the enclosed envelope to make your gift or learn more.

The Fall Field Trip allows up to 200 disadvantaged youth to participate in a three-day field trip that's both fun-filled and educational. Participants will visit a museum, a manufacturing facility, the State Capitol, a nature preserve and spend time meeting with mentors who will share their life experiences with these deserving young people. In addition, the children will spend an afternoon at the Whittleon Water Park. This will be the only travel most of these youth will have ever experienced.

Did you know? — ABC Nonprofit has an annual payroll of $754,000, contributing to the overall economic vitality of our community.

Mark your calendar — Plan to attend the ABC Nonprofit open house scheduled to take place on September 14 from 4 to 7 p.m. Meet your community's youth and see the newly renovated Learning Center.

102 — Team Up With Civic Groups

Here's an idea to build involvement and increased numbers of contributions: When you speak to civic organizations about your organization, offer to team up on a fundraising project in which your two organizations could share proceeds.

In addition to getting new volunteers working on your charity's behalf and raising money for both organizations, it's likely that some of the club's members will continue as individual donors.

103 — Load Up on Leads

Whether you're out to secure more major gifts or simply want to increase the number of annual contributors to your charity, you need new leads to generate new gifts.

Build your leads file through these and other sources:

- ✓ Others' honor rolls of contributors.
- ✓ Board and existing donor referrals.
- ✓ Seniors with no apparent heirs.
- ✓ Those who own a second residence.
- ✓ Area companies' top management.
- ✓ Those owning large amounts of real estate (check plat maps, courthouses).
- ✓ Persons on boards of directors.
- ✓ Anyone (and often relatives/ friends of anyone) who has been served by your institution or agency.

104   Turn Buyers Into Donors

Many nonprofits go beyond their primary services to sell items to the public, from artwork to souvenirs to logo-emblazoned clothing. If your organization does so, take time to evaluate existing buyers and decide how to best cultivate a donor relationship with them. Here are two important first steps to make that happen:

1. Begin by acknowledging your organization's relationship with recent buyers. Send a letter referring to and thanking them for their purchase.

2. Start to build a relationship with purchasers by offering special perks: an invitation to a reception or event, a discount on their next purchase or some other appropriate action that will help to build a relationship.

105   Grateful Patient Program Invites Thanks, Gifts

Gratitude — whether for an education, a community service, a medical procedure or other reason — is a major motivation of all philanthropic giving. This appreciation is the focus of the Memorial Medical Center Foundation's (Springfield, IL) grateful patient program.

"One of the central aims of the program is simply letting patients know that the medical center is a not-for-profit organization, and that gifts are always appreciated," says Elena Kezelis, executive director of the foundation.

Just as important, she says, is the opportunity to write a note of thanks to physicians or staff members. "People might not have returned to work or be facing insurance difficulties, and having a way to express gratitude in a non-financial way is very meaningful."

Staff distribute several thousand grateful patient brochures every year. Of those that are returned, Kezelis estimates about half include donations and half are simply messages of thanks. Donations have ranged from $10 in cash to $10,000 in stock transfers.

The brochures are stocked in all waiting rooms, and several times a year, foundation staff send them in age- and ZIP code-targeted mailings.

Involving physicians and nurse managers in the program is also key to successfully connecting grateful patients to giving opportunities, says Kezelis.

While the effort does not always end with a check in hand, she says it provides other benefits that are vitally important in their own right: "Nursing is tough, physical work, and caregivers love to be reminded that what they do is making a difference."

Source: Elena Kezelis, Executive Director, Memorial Medical Center Foundation, Springfield, IL. Phone (217) 788-4706. E-mail: Kezelis.Elena@mhsil.com

Content not available in this edition

Content not available in this edition

Stocked in all waiting rooms and sent to targeted audiences, this brochure encourages words of praise and financial gifts to the Memorial Medical Center Foundation (Springfield, IL).

106 Four Rules for Soliciting First-time Gifts

Veteran fundraisers will know that soliciting first-time gifts is different than going back to repeat contributors. There's a certain amount of rapport building and research that goes on — asking probing questions, learning more about the prospect's philanthropic background and funding interests.

Here are four rules that distinguish a first-time solicitation call from others:

1. Emphasize giving based on your perceptions of what matters most to the prospect.
2. Offer more than one gift option. (Consider a wish list of gift opportunities.)
3. Point out your hope that the donor will continue to make an annual gift.
4. Delineate the various methods of payment (e.g., credit card; monthly, quarterly or semiannual payments; electronic funds transfer) to help maximize contributions.

107 Holiday Fundraiser Raises Awareness

For the fourth year in a row, the hospice organization Gateway House of Peace (Greenfield Center, NY) will present its annual Light of Love Memorial Tree Lighting, which raises about $2,000 a year while generating awareness and friends for the organization.

The event is great for community outreach, says Joni Hanchett, president/founder. "It really motivates people to get involved with the organization."

The event takes place the first Saturday of December every year at The Barn at Mallery Street Marketplace, which helps sponsor the event by donating the laminated name tags and the tree. Four local businesses sell remembrance name tags for $2 each. Tags can also be purchased by mail. The day of the event, name tags are placed on the tree following Christmas carols sung by the local theater guild, an introduction of the organization and a prayer by a pastor from the community. Then, the tree is lit, followed by a reading of the names.

The biggest challenges of an event such as this, she says, take place the first year of the event, when it is necessary to determine the size of event you want and how much to charge for the tags, among other things. "The first year is the most time-consuming. Once you have your venue, flier, donation letter and event program in place, the next year is much easier."

Hanchett's best advice for those just starting out is to get in on an existing event that already has a following and keep the name tags at a reasonable price, which encourages people to buy more than one tag.

Source: Joni Hanchett, President/Founder, Gateway House of Peace, Greenfield Center, NY. Phone (518) 893-6443. E-mail: jhanchett@gatewayhouseofpeace.org

Luminary Sales Boost Proceeds

Selling luminary kits can be a cost-effective way to raise awareness and funds, says Joni Hanchett, president/founder, Gateway House of Peace (Greenfield Center, NY). The hospice organization hosts an annual Light of Love Memorial Tree Lighting.

"Luminary kits can be donated, costing the organization nothing," Hanchett says. "Restaurant distributors can donate white bags and your local town garage can contribute sand. After that, you will just need baggies and candles to complete the kits. In my research, I have found the going price to be about $10 for eight luminary kits. Local businesses can sell the luminaries for your organization, keeping it simple."

She adds that hospice officials plan to sell luminary kits during the annual Victorian Stroll in a neighboring town.

108 Online Giving Tips

Rather than listing a general invitation for support on your website, provide a wish list of funding projects from which contributors can choose. Change the list on a quarterly basis to measure which wish list items are most popular among your website visitors.

109 Establish a Cold Calls Committee

To broaden your base of annual support, establish an ongoing cold calls committee made up of loyal supporters willing to meet on a quarterly basis and accept responsibility for making calls between meetings.

Begin by creating a blueprint for your cold calls committee. Some of the responsibilities this committee might assume include:

- Identifying and researching prospects.
- Reviewing lists of nondonors to decide 1) cultivation/solicitation strategies and 2) who should call on whom.
- Coordinating a phonathon effort aimed at nondonors.
- Offering input on the content of marketing materials targeted to nondonors.
- Offering input on funding projects and/or wish lists aimed at nondonors.
- Hosting one or more open houses targeting nondonors.
- Coordinating a special event aimed at attracting nondonors.

110 Twitter-driven Fundraiser Brings in $10,000 in 10 Days

Nonprofit organizations across the country have had varying degrees of success in harnessing the power of Twitter (www.twitter.com) networking to bring in much-needed donations. Through these groups' trial and error, a best practices approach is emerging that can help you decide whether a Twitter-based fundraiser will work for you.

One successful group has been the ChristmasFuture Foundation (Calgary, Alberta, Canada), a nonprofit that funds projects worldwide to help erase extreme poverty. ChristmasFuture raised more than $10,000 in the 10 days before Christmas 2008 with its TweetmasFuture fundraiser, says operations manager Leif Baradoy. In all, it brought in about 7 percent of the group's annual budget.

"We've only really been around for two years as an organization, but the key to our success was that we have been able to powerfully represent ourselves through our projects," which include everything from youth arts and leadership programs in Nicaragua to funding a water sanitation project in Sierra Leone, Baradoy says.

The TweetmasFuture campaign didn't have a lot of planning involved, Baradoy says, but it did require a way to donate money online. They sent direct messages on Twitter to many of their 400-plus followers, asking them to donate and/or send out "tweets" (brief messages sent to subscribers through Twitter) about the campaign. All they had to do then was keep the word going.

Here are Baradoy's tips for a successful Twitter fundraiser:

✓ Invest in your followers: Those who have successfully raised thousands of dollars from Twitter activity all have something in common, Baradoy says — they have established a following on the social networking site for at least a year, and regularly send out useful updates (like articles, blog posts, etc. that relate to the organization's core mission) to engage their supporters in conversation. In other words, if you build trust with your social network, you build potential for a larger donation pool. "People will only share links and donate if they are convinced it is a good cause," he says.

✓ Keep it short: Any longer than 10 days is too long, Baradoy says. You don't want your campaign to become noise in the background.

✓ Give persons clear direction. In your initial message, state exactly what you would like them to do, which is to donate and retweet, Baradoy says. Don't try to say too much, as tweets are limited to 140 characters.

✓ Create a fundraiser Web page: The fundraiser should have its own Web page, and the link to that page should be included in every message you send for the event, Baradoy says. You can shorten the link through the use of computer applications like Tweetdeck, which will also help you keep track of your followers. Include your Twitter feed on that Web page, as well as publicity and links to other important aspects of your group. Make it easy for people to navigate and, of course, to donate.

✓ Use a hash tag to track the campaign: Hash tags allow Twitter users to search for all specific content related to that tag, so including one in each message related to the fundraiser is important if you want to see who's supporting you. Baradoy used #TweetmasFuture as a hash tag, but plans to shorten it for future efforts.

✓ Follow up: Keep the word going by tweeting about how much money has been raised. Chances are those will be passed on, as well. Publicly thank those who have donated and/or retweeted your messages by sending a reply on Twitter. Consistent involvement in a Twitter campaign is fundamental to success, Baradoy says.

✓ Don't just take, give back: ChristmasFuture bought some of its own online donation gift certificates and sent them to the most involved Twitter followers. They could make a donation in their name or pass the gift along to a friend.

Contact: Leif Baradoy, Operations Manager, ChristmasFuture Foundation, Calgary, Alberta, Canada. Phone (866) 629-0516. E-mail: info@christmasfuture.org

Tweeting For a Cause

Here are some sample "tweets" sent through www.twitter.com from the many staff and supporters of the ChristmasFuture Foundation (Calgary, Alberta, Canada) during a social network-driven fundraising effort in December 2008:

Kinghuang: Check out TweetmasFuture, ChristmasFuture's campaign to help end extreme poverty! http://www.christmasfuture....
4:10 PM Dec 16th, 2008 from Twitterrific

RT @UniversalGiving: Let's get this rolling! Get involved & spread the word about raising money for #tweetmasfuture http://twurl.cc/9yu
4:22 PM Dec 17th, 2008 from TweetDeck

Thank you @kinghuang @peterdietz @wiselywoven and @openzap for sharing http://bit.ly/B2aA
4:17 PM Dec 16th, 2008 from TweetDeck

#tweetmasfuture goal status: $3577 of $20,000 . 1 WEEK LEFT. http://bit.ly/3aDvSZ
8:30 PM Dec 18th, 2008 from TweetDeck

Cool fact: #tweetmasfuture has increased traffic to the site by +29% since Dec. 16th. Help spread the word about http://bit.ly/3aDvSZ
4:26 PM Dec 19th, 2008 from TweetDeck

Want to give www.christmasfuture.org a try? Go to the site, hit Receive & enter this code: eawlyyemtzep . First to use it gets it!
11:56 AM Dec 23rd, 2008 from TweetDeck

111

Encourage Volunteers to Donate to Your Cause

Encouraging new volunteers to donate to your nonprofit will set the stage for ongoing funding and get volunteers thinking about funds needed to keep your nonprofit operating.

At the Atlanta Humane Society (AHS) of Atlanta, GA, new volunteers are encouraged to donate $25 at their first training session, says Ashley Vitez, volunteer services manager. Overall, the AHS has received more than $6,000 in volunteer training donations. "The donations are to help offset expenses for training and equipment for the volunteers," says Vitez. "It also gets volunteer buy-in, because you always value something paid for more than something free."

Source: Ashley Vitez, Volunteer Services Manager, SPCA of Georgia, Inc., Atlanta, GA. Phone (404) 974-2822. E-mail: volunteer@atlantahumane.org. Website: www.atlantahumane.org

112

20 Ways to Generate Gifts, Reach First-time Donors

Looking for ways to generate new gifts from new donors? Here are 20 practical ways to do just that:

1. Ask your board to personally make a minimum number of new contacts over a specified period of time.
2. Approach users of your services/programs who don't currently give.
3. Ask current donors to invite a friend/ associate to a get-to-know-us event.
4. Identify endowment gift opportunities.
5. Publish a wish list to distribute during personal calls, on your website and in printed communications.
6. Launch a buy-a-brick campaign that includes a brick engraved with donors' names.
7. Give volunteers credit toward prizes for soliciting friends and family.
8. Set up an exhibit booth at fairs, malls and other locations to invite support.
9. Add family and friends of employees to your mailing list.
10. Identify nondonors on your mailing list and conduct a phonathon for a special funding project.
11. Get noncontributing businesses to sponsor an event, program or publication.
12. Secure a challenge grant that will match new gifts.
13. Make a staff commitment to make so many new prospect calls a week/month.
14. Begin a generational event (mother-daughter-grandmother) to invite family support.
15. Start brown-bag luncheons with a brief program and invitation to become a contributor.
16. Provide local service clubs with programs where you can share your wish list of gift opportunities.
17. Rent or exchange mailing lists.
18. Invite your constituents to organize a special event on your nonprofit's behalf.
19. Simplify the online giving process.
20. Begin testing e-appeals to select groups of names in your database.

113

Ideas Worth Considering

Looking for ways to encourage more businesses to donate to your nonprofit? Consider this:

Get together with representatives from your community's nonprofits to form a joint publicity campaign with the theme, Buy Locally, Give Locally.

The joint effort might help to build awareness and encourage a greater percentage of businesses to make first-time gifts to the nonprofits of their choice.

114

Test Appeals To Nondonors

Unsure about the best way to turn nondonors into first-time contributors? Why not test two direct mail appeals?

Try this:

1. Send one mailing to half of your nondonors that includes a wish list of specific funding projects with varying price tags.

2. Send another appeal to the remaining half asking for general support to underwrite the work of your organization (no specific projects).

Chances are the wish list appeal will produce better results. People like knowing exactly how their gifts are being used and that they are making a difference. But by testing two appeals, you will learn what works best for you.

115 Select From Among Best Reasons for Giving

What you ask for and the way in which you ask often depends on who is being asked. That's why it makes sense to develop a repertoire of compelling reasons to give — ones from which you can choose.

Most compelling reasons for giving may include but not be limited to:

✔ To establish a lasting legacy.

✔ To ensure the needs of those being served are fully met.

✔ To help build an institution or agency of regional or national repute.

✔ To help balance the budget.

✔ To gain membership in a gift club and be eligible for its accompanying benefits.

✔ To help attract and maintain talented employees.

✔ To provide the tools necessary to carry out the mission.

✔ To help reach or surpass this year's fundraising goal.

✔ To avoid being left out.

✔ To make possible a funding project that otherwise would not be available.

✔ To help meet a challenge.

✔ To maintain a record of consecutive years of giving.

116 Keep Testing New Calling Approaches

When calling on businesses for support, see if this approach sounds all too familiar: Establish rapport, make small talk, build the case for support, then make the ask for an unrestricted gift to support general operations.

Instead of the same old, same old, why not vary your approach? In addition to being a lot less boring, doing so lets you test different presentation techniques and funding opportunities to see what works best.

Here's some of what you can test:

1. **Make team calls rather than making all calls alone.** Bring a board member along on some calls one day. Try asking your mayor to accompany you on some calls. Ask a respected CEO or someone served by your organization if she/he would accompany you on three calls.

2. **Say it differently.** Deliver your presentation in various ways to see what works best and to break up the monotony. Compare the prospect's business to your organization. Share a dream of what could be. Use storytelling to build a compelling case for support.

3. **Try different "props."** Rather than leaving behind the standard annual fund brochure, try something new. Share a handful of photos that help the prospect visualize the gift opportunity. Share a brief recording.

4. **Vary your funding projects.** In addition to unrestricted gifts, define specific projects that might interest prospects more: sponsoring a particular program, enhancing a supplies budget, providing professional development funds for your employees, etc.

117 Include Tribute, Memorial Gift Options On Pledge Forms

If you would like to increase the number of memorial and/or in-tribute gifts your charity receives each year, be sure all pledge forms include that gift option along with other gift options.

In addition to specifying the name of the individual being honored or memorialized, the donor can instruct the development office to notify appropriate individuals of the gift. Portions of two pledge forms are shown below.

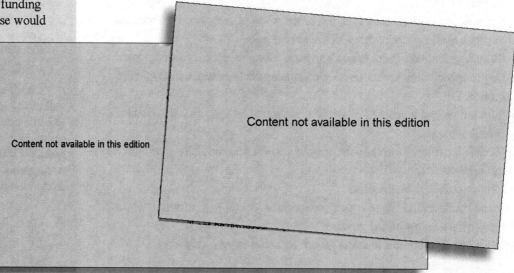

118 Identify and Shout Out Your Organization's Achievements

Donors, particularly major donors, are energized by organizations that can point to significant accomplishments. Yet we sometimes get so wrapped up in carrying out programs and fulfilling our mission that we fail to fully identify and publicize all that we are accomplishing. In fact, we sometimes even fail to realize some of our achievements.

Go through the following steps at least twice each year — or even quarterly — to identify and share your organization's achievements:

1. **Survey each department to learn all their accomplishments.** You may decide to use a form such as the example shown here, visit directly with representatives from each department or both. Whatever method you use, it's important to get department representatives to really share what they have been doing, especially since they may not recognize the significance or newsworthiness of some of their accomplishments.

2. **Assign one employee the responsibility of identifying and researching your organization's most significant achievements.** Researching includes comparing data to other organizations and benchmarking. For example, it's one thing to state, "We served 450 underprivileged youth during the past quarter." It's far more significant to say, "We served 70 percent of our city's underprivileged youth last month. That's a higher percentage than any other city our size throughout the nation."

3. **Follow a plan for getting your accomplishments out to the public.** Categorize and share your achievements with your CEO and others who meet with the public, so they can draw on particular achievements depending on circumstances. Pitch feature stories to news media outlets regarding particular achievements. Tie your stories to local and national issues to give the media even more reason to feature your organization.

Remember, it pays to toot your own horn every now and then if you want would-be donors to buy into your organization and its future accomplishments.

119 Create a Group Wish List

You may offer wish lists of needs directed to individuals, but what about a wish list targeted to groups (i.e., civic and faith-based organizations, affinity groups, corporate employees, etc.)? Graduates of colleges and universities regularly make "class gifts" in which members of a particular class are invited to support a special project. Why limit that concept? Apply it to other types of groups that may have an interest in your charity.

ACCOMPLISHMENTS SURVEY

This quarterly survey is intended to bring any and all achievements to everyone's awareness. As you complete the survey, think about your department's work during the past three months. How has employee time been focused? What has been accomplished during that time? Remember, there are no wrong answers.

The information you provide may or may not be shared with the public. The form in which it is shared will be determined by the Office of Media Relations.

Please take a few minutes to complete this survey and return it to the Office of Media Relations within the next few days. Thanks for your valuable assistance.

Your Name _____   Department_____
Phone _____   Date _____

Key areas our department has focused on over the past three months include:
1. _____   3. _____
2. _____   4. _____

In my opinion, my department's biggest recent accomplishments include:
1. _____   3. _____
2. _____   4. _____

When I think of [Name of Organization], I'm most proud of:
_____

Based on our department's work and responsibilities, here's something that others (employees and/or the public) may not realize:
_____

Can you think of any local, regional or national issues that relate directly or indirectly to accomplishments within your department? Please share them:
☐ Local issue   ☐ Regional issue   ☐ National issue
_____

Here's how our work and accomplishments are related to this issue:
_____
_____

---

120 Set Yearly Gift Club Goals

As you set your yearly fundraising goal, get specific. Set goals for each giving level or gift club. How many new $1,000 gifts do you intend to secure for that giving level? By what percentage will contributions to your $100 to $250 gift level increase next year?

Breaking down a yearly fundraising goal helps define specific actions you will need to take to achieve it.

121 Three Ways to Generate $25,000 in Gifts

Need an extra $25,000 in gift revenue this year? As you consider those fundraising strategies that might work best for your organization, put them in writing to compare ideas and select the best plan. Documenting your ideas will also help surface any weaknesses that may need to be addressed.

Here are three examples of how a charity may decide to generate an extra $25,000 in gift revenue:

1. **Coordinate a special event.** Enlist a committee of can-do volunteers who are committed to your organization and have experience at organizing fundraisers.

2. **Convince past contributors to give more.** Calculate the percentage that each of last year's donors would need to increase their giving to generate $25,000 more in gifts.

3. **Develop a plan for generating 25 new gifts of $1,000 or more.** Turn to those who already give at that level and involve them in a yearlong recruitment effort to attract 25 new donors at that level.

122 For Challenge Campaign Success, Keep It Simple, Advertise

Q. What tips do you have for someone looking to implement challenge campaigns?

"Make sure the terms of the challenge are simple — the simpler the better (e.g., the donor will match all gifts received between Jan. 1 and Feb. 15 one-to-one or the donor will match all new gifts on a one-to-one basis).

"Also, make sure you advertise it as much as possible. We sent out a postcard to announce our last challenge but didn't provide a response device, so the money came in rather slowly at first. A staff member designed a card explaining the terms of the challenge. After we began inserting that card in fund chair letters and in student calling program pledges, the money came in faster because both had business return envelopes enclosed."

Source: Joanne Davis, Director of the Annual Fund, Agnes Scott College, Decatur, GA. Phone (404) 471-5343. E-mail: jadavis@agnesscott.edu

123 Use a Challenge Gift to Encourage Credit Card Giving

In 2009, officials at Salve Regina University (Newport, RI) boosted the overall credit card giving rate by phone from 14 percent to 22 percent by attaining an alumni challenge specifically for gifts made by credit card.

"We asked the donor if she would use her gift to offer this challenge and inspire credit card giving," says Brian Kish, assistant to the vice president for advancement.

"This donor is always looking for the best way to utilize her gifts to inspire others," Kish says. "She knew that we needed to improve in this area and was more than happy to have her gift leveraged in this manner."

The challenge gift ratio was slightly under 1:1, he says.

Kish shares the script university officials used to solicit gifts for this match:

"That's great (NAME). Thank you very much. We really appreciate your gift to Salve Regina! Will that be on your MasterCard or Visa?' This illustrates the 'assumptive ask' strategy.

"If the donor says they don't want to use their credit card, the caller says: 'We have just gotten word that one of our generous alumni has offered a challenge in which she will match any gifts made to the university on a credit card. With this in mind, would you like to accept her challenge by putting your gift on a credit card tonight?'"

Kish attributes the success of the challenge to the following:

1. Donors like to know that their gift can make a difference. "When they learn that their giving can make an even larger impact if they put it on a credit card, they usually tend to be encouraged by this idea," he says.

2. It is another reason supporting the case for credit card giving. Often, we just need more reasons to inspire giving whether it is on a credit card or not.

3. It provided them with a polite way to ask again for a credit card. "Essentially a second ask," he says.

Source: Brian Kish, Assistant to the Vice President for Advancement, Salve Regina University, Newport, RI. Phone (401) 341-2151. E-mail: brian.kish@salve.edu

124   Work to Land First-time Gifts From Businesses

Want to get more gifts from members of the business community? Create gift opportunities designed to get them on board. To secure more first-time gifts from businesses:

1. Share a menu of wide-ranging sponsorship opportunities. Offer a variety of sponsorship price tags.

2. Launch a business partners program that includes any business contributing $250 or more per year. Offer members some exclusive benefits to attract their participation.

3. Form a committee of existing business contributors to assist in identifying and calling on their colleagues.

4. Convince an existing business donor to establish a challenge gift aimed at nondonor businesses. Any first-time gift will be matched by the challenger.

125   Maximizing Online Giving

On Give to the Max Day held each November, officials with GiveMN (Saint Paul, MN) ask Minnesota residents to dig deep to raise funds for favorite nonprofits online.

During the 2010 event, some 42,596 donors logged on to GiveMN.org to give $10,041,021 in 24 hours, reflecting donations as well as matching grants and prizes awarded, and bringing the total GiveMN has helped nonprofits raise in the event's two-year history to $27 million.

During its 2009 event, more than 38,000 donors logged on to the www.givemn.org website, grossing more than $14 million for 3,434 Minnesota nonprofit organizations. The 2010 event included the goal to engage 40,000 people to give to their favorite Minnesota charities.

"The 2009 event was an auspicious start for GiveMN, which was created to help Minnesotans discover, support and directly engage with organizations that match their giving goals," says Dana Nelson, executive director of GiveMN.

Nelson offers the following tips for driving your online fundraising efforts:

✓ **Get personal.** Answer the question: What inspires you about the cause and the organization? Make your appeal and story personal and highlight your motivations for asking for funds. Sharing your passion for the cause will inspire donors to contribute, too.

✓ **Be visual.** Nothing helps more than a vivid photograph or a compelling video about your cause, featuring interviews and insights about the impact that a donor will have.

✓ **Give it a deadline.** Whether it's a matching grant that expires or a goal to raise a certain amount of money in a given time frame, give donors a reason to give now.

✓ **Make it a contest.** Encourage donors to start a contest to see who can raise the most for your organization. They can grow mustaches, have a Wii tournament, or do anything else they enjoy — all to support your cause!

✓ **Show specifics.** Show exactly how you will use a $10, $20 or $100 gift. Describe how giving more will result in more or better impact.

Source: Dana Nelson, Executive Director, GiveMN.org, Saint Paul, MN.
Phone (202) 595-3385. E-mail: dana@givemn.org. Website: www.givemn.org

126   Active Committees Give Way To Increased Support

It's a basic fund development premise: Meaningful volunteer involvement results in financial contributions. So, doesn't it make sense that the more you involve volunteers in meaningful ways, the more you will eventually increase both annual and major gifts?

Here's a checklist of some of the types of committees and advisory groups that can exist as ways to expand volunteer involvement in fund development:

❑ Board Development Committee
❑ Annual Fund Committee
❑ Major Gifts Committee
❑ Campaign Steering Committee
❑ Planned Gifts Committee
❑ Planning Task Force
❑ Phonathon Committee
❑ Special Events Committees
❑ Auxiliary
❑ Nominating Committee
❑ Public Relations Committee
❑ Strategic Planning Committee
❑ Rating and Screening Committee
❑ Special Gifts Committee
❑ Grants & Foundations Committee
❑ Community Campaign Committee
❑ Membership Committee
❑ Giving Clubs Committees
❑ Memorial/In Tribute Gifts Committee
❑ Endowment Committee
❑ Awards Committee

Eight Strategies to Increase Returns On Direct Mail Appeals

While there may be no magic bullet when it comes to writing direct mail appeals, development officials can take specific steps to boost return rates on fundraising letters, says fundraising consultant Kenneth Hoffman (Lexington, MA).

Hoffman bases his assessment on 30-plus years of experience in the nonprofit community, including nearly 25 years as a consultant on fundraising programs directed at foundation, individual and corporate donors.

His primary tip? "If you only do one thing, make sure your letter is personalized with a handwritten postscript. It can be general or very specific (e.g., 'It was great to see you at...'), but it should be handwritten."

Hoffman shares eight tips for creating the perfect annual appeal letter:

1. Consider and determine the explicit purpose of your letter. Is it cultivation, prospecting, renewal? Hoffman says it isn't necessary to segment your letters to each of those different audiences, but it is imperative to think about how your letter relates to each of those audiences.

2. Answer the four questions of any fundraising appeal. Who are you? How much do you want? What do you want it for? Why should the donor give it to you? Hoffman says the second question throws people off the most. "Culturally, it's felt to be a violation of privacy." Hoffman says it isn't necessary to list specific amounts for people to give, but it is important to create a scale of giving. "People need to know how much you're trying to raise in total, to put their giving in perspective."

3. Take real care with your language. It defines whether the gift you receive will be restricted or unrestricted. Rather than describing a specific program and making it seem as if the money will go directly to that program, say something like, "For example, we do A, B and C." This will ensure that the gift will be unrestricted.

4. Talk to your chief executive. This ensures you can share his/her perspective on where the organization is going and what he/she wants to say.

5. Don't use implied threats. Hoffman says tactics such as, "Send money, or we'll go out of business," or trying to raise money to retire a deficit are hopeless causes that diminish the donor's confidence in your organization.

6. Collect other people's annual appeals. This will help you to determine what you like and what you don't like, which will help you construct your next appeal. Hoffman also recommends never reading your prior year's appeal, as doing so will only get you stuck in the same mind set.

7. Don't put a stamp on the return envelope. Research shows it does not impact outcome.

8. Follow up quickly. Don't forget to thank your donors for the money — quickly. Hoffman says the point of the letter is to make it easy for the donor to donate. "Basically, you want to give them an envelope to stuff full of money." The easier you make it for them to do that, the greater your returns will be.

Source: Kenneth Hoffman, Fundraising Consultant, Lexington, MA. Phone (781) 274-7337. E-mail: khoffman@igc.org

Four Tried-and-true Steps To Annual Appeal Funds

Fundraising consultant Kenneth Hoffman (Lexington, MA) says the most common mistake writers of annual appeal letters make is forgetting that the letter is an ongoing, ritual communication.

The formula for making appeal letters work is very basic, Hoffman says, and involves just four elements:

- **Paragraph One.** Here we are. Send money.
- **Paragraph Two.** This is what we did with the money you sent before.
- **Paragraph Three.** This is what we're going to do with the money you send now.
- **Paragraph Four.** Here we are. Send money.

To that end, he says he recommends that appeal letters be kept to one page. "I've yet to see a convincing argument for two pages."

128 Equate a Modest Gift With Everyday Purchases

Approaches you take for first-time gifts are obviously different from those you would take with existing contributors, particularly those who give at more generous levels. But to convince nondonors to make that first-time gift, think about comparing a specific asking amount to everyday purchases. It's a common approach, but one that many nonprofits overlook when targeting nondonors with a direct mail appeal or during a telesolicitation effort.

This comparison approach also makes sense if your goal is to increase the giving participation rate among those on your mailing list. If you have a pool of 10,000 constituents, for example, it takes 100 new gifts to increase your participation rate by 1 percent. To do that, you might want to ask for a $10 gift — to be used for a specific purpose — and compare the gift amount to any of these everyday purchases:

✓ Ten lottery tickets.
✓ Two or three greeting cards.
✓ Three cups of specialty coffee.
✓ Less than 10 days of Internet service.
✓ Two meals at a fast-food restaurant.
✓ Two tickets at a movie theater.

129 Create a Handout Geared to Area Businesses

When calling on businesses in your community and service area, it's important to have a marketing piece that speaks directly to them and their specific organization. Printed information that could easily be tailored to business contacts includes:

✓ A list of all businesses that contributed during the past fiscal year (possibly arranged by giving clubs or levels).

✓ Messages that speak to your organization's impact on the local economy (i.e., number of employees, payroll, etc.).

✓ Brief testimonials from respected business leaders (both large and small businesses).

✓ Perks (for businesses) for giving at various levels.

✓ Profiles of partnerships that exist between your organization and businesses.

✓ Messages about how your organization positively impacts the quality of life in your community.

✓ A separate list of businesses that sponsored various programs throughout the past year.

✓ Examples of how your organization participates as a corporate citizen (i.e., chamber member, representation on boards, etc.).

130 Encourage Contributions From Churches, Synagogues

Some nonprofit organizations have ties to a particular religion. Others do not. In either case, you have to decide whether faith-based organizations might support your cause with annual contributions.

If you decide it's worth your time to encourage giving among religious groups, you might want to consider these approaches:

✓ List faith-based organizations as a separate category in your annual honor roll of contributors.

✓ Explore the possibility — and consider the appropriateness — of a friendly competition among congregations to raise funds for your charity.

✓ Provide religious organizations with bulletin inserts that make the case for supporting your cause.

✓ Encourage your organization's existing contributors to approach their church or synagogue for support on your behalf.

✓ Offer to provide faith-based organizations with a presentation about your agency and its work.

✓ Meet with your community's clergy group to discuss your cause and the most appropriate approaches for seeking support.

131 Gifts-in-kind Can Lead to Cash Gifts

Keep this thought in mind: sometimes it's smarter to ask a potential contributor for something other than money. Asking a prospect for a gift-in-kind that may not be perceived as costly is one way to begin to build a relationship with a donor that will one day lead to cash gifts.

Review your list of nondonor businesses. Ask yourself what each business offers or manufactures or sells that you could use. A service? A product? Their employees' time? Specialized knowhow? Then approach the business with a legitimate request for how a gift of that service, product or knowhow could genuinely benefit your cause.

You will find that this approach tends to be less threatening to some businesses — and more affordable from their point of view. Plus, such gift-in-kind contributions will begin paving the way for cash down the road.

132 Ask Questions That Measure Understanding, Interest

Do you ever meet with prospects who come across as the "silent type" — saying little the entire time?

Whenever meeting one-on-one with a prospect, if the person doesn't ask questions along the way, try forcing responses to learn more about where he/she stands.

Here are two examples of questions designed to help uncover a prospect's understanding and/or interest about a particular project:

✓ What interests you most about what I've just described?

✓ I would be interested in knowing your opinions about this program or, for that matter, anything about our agency.

133 Do You Have a Plan for Making New Friends?

Because of the constant pressure to raise gifts now, taking steps to establish new friendships with persons who may not contribute for a year or two doesn't get the attention it should. That's why it's important to develop a written plan that regularly introduces your organization to new prospects.

Spend some time with the development team to identify how you can best go about establishing new relationships with would-be donors. Come up with a yearlong written plan that includes quantifiable objectives — not unlike the example below. Once your plan is in place, you will find that the time required to create new relationships rarely robs time from immediate fundraising pressures.

2011-12 Prospect Introduction Measures	
New Intros	Action To Be Taken
144	Each development officer (3) is expected to make no less than four new (face-to-face) acquaintances each month.
30	Increase the number of new attendees to the Winter Gala by 30 individuals.
14	Host two on-site receptions that each attract seven new guests.
300	Increase the mailing list by 2 percent (new names).
5	Make introductions with five new foundations throughout the year.
36	Host monthly executive breakfasts that include three new attendees per breakfast (on average).
529	Total New Contacts

134 Make It Easy for Businesses to Solicit Their Employees

When people know what's expected of them, they're much more likely to pitch in and help. That's why you should make it easy for business owners and top management to invite their employees to support your charity. Here's what's involved:

1. Identify key business contacts who are already supportive of your organization — owners and top managers.

2. Develop a user-friendly packet of materials you can take to those individuals. It should include a simple outline of ways they can invite their employees to give to your organization, a sample script for the contact to put in a pitch when meeting with employees and sufficient brochures, pledge forms and return envelopes to be distributed to all employees.

3. Once you get one or two businesses that have successfully invited their employees to support your cause, bring those business heads along when you meet with and attempt to convince other businesses to participate. Ask them to give testimonials.

4. Identify perks tailored to these new business partners and any of their employees who make contributions.

135 Develop a Process for Setting Prospect Appointments

If your job includes making calls on would-be donors, it's important to religiously schedule appointments in advance.

To do so effectively, craft an introductory letter that you mail out one week prior to calling for the appointment. Your letter should grab the prospect's attention and set the stage for your appointment-setting call. The last sentence of your letter should emphasize that you will be calling within the next few days to schedule a visit.

GOAL: TO SCHEDULE 15 PROSPECT VISITS PER WEEK		
Week One	Week Two	Week Three
Send 20 prospect letters	Schedule appointments	Meet with 15 prospects

Plan to send out at least one-third more letters each week than needed to fill your weekly schedule. For example, if you want to schedule 15 calls (on average) per week, send letters to 20 people each week, assuming not everyone will choose to meet with you.

By repeating this cycle on an ongoing basis, you will be able to establish a solid habit of appointment setting with new prospects.

136 Evaluate and Rejuvenate Your Top Sales Points

Chances are you have several key points you always stress when making prospect calls. But have you used those same selling points so often that you're barely conscious of what's coming out of your mouth? Maybe those key points — or the way in which you present them — could use some pizzazz. Or maybe what you thought should be your key selling points really aren't so impressive any more.

To evaluate and rejuvenate your charity's top selling points, complete this exercise:

1. In a staff meeting, ask everyone to list their top one-liners. Then discuss each one. Is it really that impressive? Could wording it differently make it more powerful?

2. After discussing each sales point, attempt to prioritize them, discussing why one point should take precedence over another. The process of doing this will help justify the use of each point as a sales tool.

3. Once the points have been prioritized, conduct a brainstorming session, coming up with new sales points that aren't on the list. Anything goes. Once you've completed that, discuss which, if any, of the new sales points should take their place among the previous list.

Taking the time to review key sales points will breathe new life into your fundraising presentations.

137 Are $25 Gifts a Waste of Your Fundraising Time?

Granted, all of the most important fundraising principles emphasize the importance of focusing on major gifts. No doubt about it, your development staff should be focusing an ample amount of time on ways to generate big gifts. So why even focus, say, 15 percent of your time on seeking new gifts in the $25 range? Here's why:

1. If you haven't had a long history of fundraising and your donor constituency is relatively small, it's important to increase your pool of regular (annual) contributors.

2. Most major donors give at far lesser levels prior to making more generous gifts.

3. Consider the lifetime value of a contributor: If you can get a first-time gift of even $25 that becomes habitual, the multiplier effect comes into play.

138   Nondonor Focus Groups Offer Opportunity to Give

If one of your goals is to broaden your base of annual support, here's a concept worth executing: Conduct a series of focus group sessions among nondonors. Here's how it might work:

1. Select any number of nondonors on your mailing list and assemble them into groups of say, 30. Come up with 10 groupings. You may choose to vary the characteristics of each group (i.e., age, sex, financial capability, etc.), since this is a test and having various types of groups may yield varying results.

2. Schedule 10 different hour-long sessions — one for each group. Here again, you may wish to vary the timing of each session to measure which produced the highest attendance.

3. Draft a letter from you CEO (and possibly signed by your board chair as well) that explains how you are trying to better understand perceptions about your organization from members of the community and that you would like them to attend an hour-long discussion to invite their input. (They need not know that you are inviting only nondonors to participate.)

4. Incorporate some "drawing card appeal" aspect into your invitation as a way of motivating them to participate (i.e., free tickets to an event, dinner with your CEO and board chair immediately following the discussion session, etc.).

5. Send the invitation letter to each of the 10 groups two weeks prior to their scheduled sessions. The invitations are being sent to 30 people knowing that it's likely only a third (or less) may choose to participate.

6. When it's time for a focus group session to take place and you know how many from a group indicated they plan to attend, ask some of your organization's closest friends (contributing board members or volunteers who are considered "insiders") to sit in as participants of the group. The reason for "stacking the deck" is to help soften any negative comments with positive ones as the sessions take place and also to help facilitate discussion.

7. When the session is under way, pose as many as 10 questions to the group that seek their input regarding their perceptions of your organization and its work. You may even choose to go around the room to help encourage responses from everyone in attendance.

8. Although your intent should be to genuinely listen to people's perceptions — both good and bad — that will help you to make internal improvements, at least one of the final questions should address giving: "Having shared your honest input with us today, I would like to ask each of you what would we need to do in order for you to begin contributing to our organization — regardless of gift amount — on an annual basis?"

9. Follow up each session with a personal letter of thanks and a message that you will be arranging a one-on-one appointment to follow up on the opinions they so generously shared. Then, when you meet, determine if the time is right to solicit a gift or if more cultivation will be needed.

How many gifts (and at what amounts) — based on your investment of time — will it take for this focus group process to have been a success? Only you can answer that question. But consider this: Anyone who took the time to attend a session has now been engaged in the life of your organization and is far more likely to make that first-time contribution.

Focus Group Questions For Nondonors

1. When you hear the words [name of your organization], what thoughts come to mind?

2. What, in your opinion is [name of organization] best known for?

3. What do you think [name of organization] does best?

4. In what ways do think [name of organization] has "missed the mark?" Where are we weak, or what mistakes have we made?

5. What, in your opinion, should we do to fix those problems or weaknesses?

6. If you were in charge of [name of organization], what would be your top priority?

7. If [name of organization] were to receive a $1 million gift, how would you direct its use?

8. How can [name of organization] become a more valuable asset to this community (or region)?

9. In what ways has [name of organization] touched or impacted your life?

10. Having shared your honest input with us today, I would like to ask each of you, what would we need to do for you to begin contributing to our organization — regardless of gift amount — on an annual basis?

Lightning Source UK Ltd.
Milton Keynes UK
UKOW01f0821020813

214783UK00006B/148/P